ENIGMA
Volume One

UNIVERSITY OF EXETER
CREATIVE WRITING
SOCIETY

FOREWORD

I am delighted to welcome you to the University of Exeter Creative Writing Society's inaugural print Journal, ENIGMA.

Launched in February 2019, ENIGMA provides an innovative platform and voice to the creative output at the University of Exeter, publishing poetry, fiction, nonfiction and script.

It has been an absolute pleasure to direct an editorial team that has grown from a small group of ten at our launch, to an established and confident team of sixteen. It is thanks to their hard work, drive and dedication that I am proud to say our published submissions have quadrupled in the 2019/20 academic year.

Within Volume One, ENIGMA celebrates experimental style, content and form. Altogether it encompasses Exeter's finest writing on love, family, relationships, injustice, death, suffering, growing up, health, purpose, religion, myth, science, nature, and the arts.

I would like to thank our **Print Director Susannah Hearn** and **Print Assistant Ed Bedford**, whose hard work made this print Journal possible.

Thank you to all the Editors for their continued support and enthusiasm in helping others improve their writing. Thank you to the Creative Writing Society Committee for leading a variety of workshops and for being a source of guidance to our members. And finally, thank you to the writers, whose creativity and imagination inspires us all.

Emma Blackmore, Journal Director

ACKNOWLEDGMENTS

Editorial Team 2019/2020

Print Director
Susannah Hearn

Journal Director
Emma Blackmore

Print Assistant
Ed Bedford

Assistant Editor
Aayushi Jain

Assistant Editor
Ellie Gibson

Assistant Editor
Sarah Jackson

Fiction Editor
Zach Mayford

Fiction Editor
Juliette Tulloch

Fiction Editor
Susannah Hearn

Fiction Editor
Isabel Potter

Nonfiction Editor
Emily Wilson

Nonfiction Editor
Rosana Wardle

Script Editor
Daisy Pepperell

Poetry Editor
Ed Bedford

Poetry Editor
Zebulun O'Regan

Poetry Editor
Claudia Kelley

Poetry Editor
Abbie Walker

Poetry Editor
Natalie Tongue

Editorial Team 2018/2019

Journal Director
Mubanga Mweemba

Creative Assistant
Natalie Tongue

Poetry Editor
George Richards

Poetry Editor
James Wijesinghe

Fiction Editor
Susannah Hearn

Fiction Editor
Katie Rivers

Nonfiction Editor
Emma Blackmore

Nonfiction Editor
Ben Bampton

Assistant Editor
Claudia Kelley

Assistant Editor
Zach Mayford

With special thanks to:
The University of Exeter Creative Writing Society
Committee 2019/2020:

President — Leah Frape
Vice President — Jacob Bradshaw
Treasurer — Ed Bedford
Social Secretary — Lily Proctor

ENIGMA was supported by the University of Exeter
Students' Guild Annual Fund.

CONTENTS

Love

Family

Relationships

Injustice

Death

Suffering

Growing Up

Health

Purpose, Decisions

Religion

Myth

Science

Nature

Art, Music, Language, Literature

Trigger Warnings
* sexual abuse
** physical or emotional abuse
† offensive language
†† suicide or self-harm
‡ substance abuse
‡‡ violence or murder

LOVE

A Template of Stories

Penny Senanarong

when it began PERSON A SAW PERSON B as a
fantasy made flesh, an angel descended when it began
the sunlight was kissing their skin and lips when it
began the firefly lights flew in circles — it was dizzying
when it began the light was garish and burned,
belonging to an anglerfish when it began light is
incorporeal unreal untrue: hence false when it began it
ended and when it ended PERSON A SAW PERSON
B

For You

Toby Brooks

And I don't remember the cold, I remember the sun's spotlight.
And I don't remember fighting the wind, I remember the marks that we left on the sand.

I don't remember the long wait either, I only remember the games we played.
I remember the feeling in my chest,
Not the pain in my head.

But I remember when we got back; how your eyes were all consuming,
How your smile could have saved me.

Now I remember watching you go, the glare in the carriage window
That stole away my favourite view.

Not knowing when I'll have another chance
To get lost in that outrageous glance.
That's the hardest part.

And now the sun pushes on my headache and makes it worse,
And the wind tries to knock me from my aching legs.

A song, a jumper, an image effortlessly
Pulls me back to thinking of you.

I'll run home and surround myself with pictures of you,
To find that I'm comforted only by your image.

Coldness clenches every crevasse of my body on nights
like this
As I await the harsh resolve of the sunrise.

I tried to bandage myself with your scarf,
To stop my memories from pouring out of me.

I clung to my phone because when it lights up it has a
picture of you
And I read over your reassuring promises.

Maybe I'll say something we both know I don't mean,
And let the part of me we both hate show itself for a brief
moment

And it'll shadow us for the next day or so
Then I'll make a shallow promise that it won't happen
again.

The reality we share has nothing to do with daffodils,
roses or summer's days.
It is the song we found together, the painting you made
for me and the poem I wrote
For you.

Toasted

Sofia Miah

You whispered to me once
That the sunlight looked so good on my skin,
Toasted with a tint of caramel,
Your favourite sight to wake up to
In the morning.

In an attempt to express my appreciation
For that comment,
I lovingly made you eggy French toast
Toasted with a tint of caramel,
You called it your second favourite
Sight to wake up to in the morning.

I thought about what time of day
Looked best on you,
And concluded it was the golden hour
The hazy, soft pinkness that
Precedes the sunset,
That clothes the muscles on
Your back in a warm glow
Giving me an exact outline
To trace with my lips.

I tried to take a picture of
That time of day,
To capture the vibrancy and

The quietness with which it appears
And show you what I mean,
But its gentle presence,
Like yours,
Was short-lived.
The darkness of the night
Seeped out too soon.

I am learning to live with this,
And I hope that one day
When I wake up
And gaze in the mirror,
I'll see myself
Toasted with a tint of caramel,
And be able to call it,
My favourite sight in the morning,
Instead of just yours.

Origami

Zebulun O'Regan

we climb up the cuttings
      in the hill. chalk under nails,
your laughter plunging into
                  the sun.
          cigarette
dangles from the corner of your lip,
curling its
      origami smoke.

i say look at the view,
     you say you're already looking
         at it — your half-baked smile
waning

     over the horizon, as pavements below
crackle
with chalk: kids' games; strangers' names,
     all swoon
         as the
            day
blushes into pastel.

The Guide Book For Bad Cyclists

Clementine Venn

They say love is blind,
As blind as a girl cycling through the rain with no helmet on,
And that was me,
When I first lay eyes on you.
A girl cycling through a hurricane.

I was never good with directions. But
when you traced a map between my hips,
I knew the only right turn was the one to you.

For a while, we kept the outside out.
I wrote in big letters: NO INTRUDERS ALLOWED, signed
with the stain of my red lipstick. We hid
underneath the layers of our tremendous fort
and I felt safe enveloped in your arms.

But someone should have told me,
that all the love in the world,
cannot fix a broken soul. Yours
was the most beautiful wreckage,
my hands had ever managed to replenish.

For a while, it was as blissful as soft white sheets and warm cups of tea.
I was so caught up in you — an impossible knot — one

arm gripping you,
begging you not to go. The other grasping at the string
wrapped around my throat.

I was walking on a tightrope to get to you and as I took
my final
step, you cut me loose. And then you became the glue,
that put the parts of me back together.

You kept my heart in your back pocket and
occasionally, when it would stop beating,
your lips would venture down through the caves
and sip from my tepid pool.
My heart throbs manically in its denim cage once more.

They say love is blind — but is it deaf too?
Because every night when you told me you loved me,
I was sure it was true. You planted
sunflower seeds within my heart, but I cried all the water
away.
Now they are rotten and falling apart.

Tear-stained papers scribbled with the faintest evidence
of your name,
tiny black hairs resting on my pillow case,
the empty bottle of your favourite aftershave,
the image of your face slowly slipping away into the arms
of yesterday.

My love was blind,
as blind as a girl cycling in the rain with no helmet on.
But if she kept on cycling through that storm,
eventually she would fall,

— searching for a love —
that was there within herself all along.
Now, I never forget to put my helmet on.

FAMILY

Leaving Surigao on a Shorthaul Plane

Pip Uden

On a necklace made of common shells from the ferry place in
Cebu,
I twisted every bead on plastic string
as we hopped *over thirty islands*. Well, that's what Mum said.
We wheeled our cases off the runway.
After I hugged her sisters and played with their daughters, I
heard
something about *'mapagbiro'* sons. Then, I exchanged waves,
smiles
and Pisos for chocolate worse than home's.
And when I turned seven, I tried
to catch the odd *'Salamat!'* when I helped cousins to fish,
watching lips haggle under the orange market lights which
were melting the sugary *iskranbol*,
before the other kids' whining eyes — and mine, too!
Mum held my toasted arms up,
her friends rambled on by the river whilst I scraped for
some syllables and coconut strings; in time I gathered
courage and asked for help. When I opened my mouth,
half of my family tree started to rot.

Half of my family tree, started to rot when I opened my
mouth — I gathered courage and asked for help,
for some syllables and coconut strings. In time,
her friends rambled on by the river whilst I scraped.
Mum held my toasted arms up
before the other kids' whining eyes, and mine, too—
which were melting the sugary *iskranbol*,
watching lips haggle under the orange market lights

to catch the odd *'Salamat.'* When I helped cousins to fish,
and when I turned seven, I tried
smiles and Pisos, for chocolate worse than home's,
I heard something about *'mapagbiro'* sons, then I exchanged waves
after I hugged her sisters and played with their daughters.
We wheeled our cases off the runway.
As we hopped over thirty islands — well that's what Mum said—
I twisted every bead on plastic string
on a necklace, made of common shells from the ferry place in Cebu.

The Comedown

Frances Nolan

A huge puddle had formed outside the door. The rain came down in diagonal lines. The trees opposite me shuddered under the weight of the water. It was brutal. It had been raining for four, maybe five hours now. And we're talking hard, torrential rain. I peered up at the sky through the pub door's window. It was grey, thick with water, and covered the street in a gloomy, dull light. I turned away from the window.

It wasn't much lighter inside the pub. We hadn't pulled the curtains and a few of the light bulbs had blown when Tom had flicked the switch. It felt like we were stuck in the apocalypse. The place smelled musty; the air felt thick in the nostrils. I would've opened a window to get a fresh flow of air into the room if it didn't mean also letting in the torrents of water. Except for the thin coating of dust that wrapped itself around everything in the room, it was pretty much the same as the last time I was here. I shook the thought away.

My eyes landed on Tom, who was sitting under one of the few functioning lightbulbs in the corner of the room. He had paused from reading the mass of paperwork in front of him to look at me. He raised his eyebrows as if to say 'when are you going to start doing something useful?' We were the only two in the pub. We were probably the only two who'd been here in the past ten months, except maybe a metre man. Red seats rung around the room, the bar centre stage. On the ceiling beams hung horseshoes, old leather boots and a fishing rod. Coasters lay scattered on the tables and a sole pint glass hid abandoned on a windowsill. I pursed my lips and turned to the bar. What did we still need to do? Wipe tables, sort glasses, restock the bar? There was a leak somewhere in the roof which needed patching, and most of the wood in the building was unstable. There was also the chunk of paperwork to negotiate but that was a little beyond me. I decided sorting glasses was something I could manage without fucking up, and headed behind the bar.

Tom and I had always been different, although we did look pretty similar. Brown hair, thick, tough eyebrows and sad pasty skin. His beard was better than mine though, it had to be said. It was kind of poetic. He was the one with his shit together. He'd been the one to organise the funeral, to arrange the wake. I was the one who fell apart. Just like my facial hair, a little bit weak. The wake had been held in the pub, of course, and it had been absolutely packed, of course. My dad was a big deal in the neighbourhood. People started caring about you when you gave them cheap alcohol. Mum had made a big ceremony of hanging his photo behind the bar. People clapped, people cried. Everyone expected his boys to keep the place up and running, to keep the spirit of it alive. We didn't. Instead Dad had been hanging on the wall for ten months, watching his life's work slowly be buried under particles of dust.

A drip fell from the ceiling. The torrent of rain had obviously wormed its way into the building and was collecting somewhere on the ceiling above. A problem for later. I looked at the crates of glasses that were stacked precariously behind the bar. Wine glasses, pint glasses, half pints, whiskey glasses, champagne flutes, all sorts. My dad was a lot of things but organised was not one of them. At least I didn't have to wade through the hundreds of pages of paper like Tom. I didn't understand a lot of what was in those documents, but I knew that there were holes in the numbers. I felt grateful for a moment to have an older brother who simply assumed the difficult jobs. I crouched down and began sorting through the glasses.

When I was fourteen Tom had given me my first beer. I had had sips here and there, of course, but never a whole pint to myself. It had been a rainy day, like today, and we were at home, lounging about after school. Mum and Dad would have been down at the pub, welcoming the first of the regulars for the night. He'd handed me the cool glass bottle and said 'get it down ya.' I'd tipped the green glass to my lips, heart pulsing and hands sweaty. I didn't want to disappoint. The beer had escaped the bottle faster than I was expecting and it had slammed into the back of my throat. It had fizzed up my sinuses and out of my nose, dripping onto the carpet. Tom had laughed and walked away, but I didn't touch another beer until three years later when he taught me how to pull a pint. From seventeen to nineteen there was rarely a night where I wasn't in this pub, whether it was behind the bar or slumped on it. After university I branched out a little. Whiskey, Valium, eventually cocaine.

A glass slipped through my fingers and shattered across the grimy floor.

"We're supposed to be cleaning up this mess, not making one," came his voice. I didn't reply. Sitting down on the bar floor, listening to the steady *drip drip* of water,

I closed my eyes and sighed. I knew today would be hard, but I didn't think it would be quite like this. Tom and I hadn't spoken in over a month, and other than the time I called him drunk from the airport asking for a lift, we hadn't seen each other since the wake. I'd jetted out of the UK pretty quickly after Dad died. Yeah it was selfish, but it was so hard being places where he'd been. Visiting mum would mean visiting the wife he'd never touch again. Going to the pub meant drinking where he'd never drink again. Time is not our friend. It is fickle, and a bitch. I could hold my breath and count back to ten and then the bar would be thick with the sound of Van Morrison, the clack of pool balls. There would be the smell of spilt beer, of the dishwasher, of smokers coming in from the cold. It was so easy to imagine. And yet the fact that my dad would never speak again, never laugh again, never blink again was nonsensical. It did not compute. He died ten months ago. He was and now he never will be. It didn't make sense then, and it doesn't make sense now.

I stood up and stepped over the glass. *Crunch*. Drops of water from the ceiling turned steadily into a stream. The buckets and the broom were out the back. As I walked to go and find them, I contemplated popping a Valium. I definitely had some in my bag and it would help, for sure. Just being around Tom was putting me on edge. But I didn't really want to. Being here felt like a comedown. Maybe it was the weather, maybe it was something else, but I felt more sober now, surrounded by stale beer kegs and dusty bottles of Glenfiddich, than I had in the past year. I had only been back in the country for a couple weeks, but it felt like I'd never left. I'd spent four months in South America, two months in Italy and the rest of my time dossing around in Spain. I didn't remember a lot of it. I guess I had my dad to thank for that. He always said that he wanted me to do something fun with the inheritance. 'Don't you dare spend this repaying university debt,' he'd said, although somehow I don't think almost killing myself with pills was quite what he had in mind.

Tom, as far as I know, had never seen the appeal of drugs. Even when he'd give me beer and get drunk at the pub he'd be sensible about it. Water before bed, best not to drink after 1am. When he realised the path I was going down he was irate.

"Dumb son of a bitch is going to be dead at twenty seven," he'd told mum.

I felt the unmistakable tinge of shame settle over me. Over half the money Dad had left me was gone, spent in back alleys in Naples. No one ever mentioned my habits to Dad. He knew I liked to drink, of course. If Tom gave me my bachelors in drinking, Dad gave me my doctorate. Not that he was an alcoholic, but my dad had a certain kind of respect for alcohol. Over the years at the bar he'd seen it tear people apart, but also create friendships and bonds that are still strong today. He understood the power behind a couple of pints shared between friends.

I located the bucket and the broom and walked them back to the crime scene. The floor beneath the leak was now sodden, and the ceiling was stained and damp. I put the bucket into position. Since I'd been out the back Tom had arranged the mess of papers into a tight pile and was standing at the door, peering out at the rain as I had done earlier. The water had waged another assault and had began to seep under the door, staining the carpet a deep red.

"We should probably put some towels down," I said.

He didn't answer. I shrugged to myself and collected the shards of glass into a pile before leaning the broom against the bar counter. I tapped my fingers together. Maybe I would get that Valium after all. I stood for a moment and listened to the downpour outside and the steady drum of water hitting the bucket.

"Why did you leave?"

I stopped tapping my fingers and looked over at Tom. He still had his back to me. I was blindsided. He'd never asked me outright about my time away. He had made it pretty obvious that he wasn't happy with how I'd handled the last ten months, but he'd never spoken about it.

"What?"

"You heard me. Do you know what you did to Mum?"

I had no answer for him.

"She fell apart and I fell apart and where were you? Getting high in some club bathroom in Barcelona." He turned around. "Do you think Dad would be impressed, huh? To hear you've thrown all his money at coke and booze."

"I don't do coke anymore."

"Shut the fuck up. Look at this place." He threw up his hands. "How is this what it's become? How could you let this happen? Did you for one moment of your little adventure stop to think of me, or Mum, or Dad? Was it that easy to forget about him?"

"Hey just because I was away doesn't mean this place had to go to shit. Don't put that on me."

"Oh what you were expecting to come home and find I'd quit my job and taken on this place, huh? I'm just waiting for you to come back to the real world. You're delusional."

He walked a few steps closer until he was two metres from me. The stream of water coming from the ceiling was between us, its sound struggling to drown out our voices.

"When did I ask you to quit your job? I'm just saying this isn't my fault. I had my own shit to sort out."

"Oh yeah, typical. Your own shit. Do you ever think of anyone but yourself? You're the most selfish bastard I've ever seen."

"People grieve in different ways, Tom."

"Is that what grief looks like? White powder and pills aren't gonna bring him back."

And with that the ceiling, rotten from years of neglect and water damage and heavy from the rain, fell through, a heavy oak table from the floor above crashing and splintering to the floor between us.

We both jumped backwards, hands shielding our faces. Breathed, waited a moment, then looked down. The table was a wooden mess on the floor. The stream of water had now subsided to a drip, the last of the puddle trickling down onto the table. We said nothing for a while.

Tom moved first. He disappeared behind the bar and out to the back. A few minutes later he came back carrying a large beer keg, and set it up on the bar counter. He pulled out two grimy glasses and, after wiping them briefly on his T-shirt, poured two pints. I moved over to the bar, and he handed me one. The perfect ratio of beer to head.

"Cheers," I muttered, and took a sip. It tasted warm and metallic. Fucking terrible. But we sipped it all the same. I moved over to one of the windows and pulled back the thick curtains. Some dull sunlight streamed in, illuminating the thousands of particles disturbed by the movement of the fabric. I looked back at Tom, standing under the photo of our dad.

"Cheers," he replied.

I turned back to the window and the rain eased off.

(Csilla)g

Adel Takacs

("Csilla" is a Hungarian name derived from the word "csillag",
meaning star)

These are the secrets I cannot keep:
How she bends over the world to plant a goodnight's
kiss,
That her scarred arms hide underneath kitchen cloths,
behind books and Sunday's wishful thinking. The sunrise
drips from her tired back in the morning, Dawn makcs
her coffee and time flakes
And when the night falls, she scatters into beams.
I sleep on her curved spine
No trace of fret on her lips — I don't know where she
puts it,
Yet she hides, always behind the regimes that once tied
her hands
There are ghosts that can touch her, I can see them in the
patchwork of her iris
Spits of green and gold — a decoy for what the world
could never hold.
In the dark she asks, *"what's in a name?"*
"Nothing if no one says it." It's easy for you, and me but
There are tyrant potters in her brain — took her years to
break the mould.
Rearranged, shoved in her pockets but the pieces still
poke through, from time to time—
She stands tall, but the sun always casts a shadow.

Warm Winter, in her secret garden,
Work shoes and afternoon naps
A foreign language, a flowerbed for maps
She's on her knees, violets growing around her soft limbs
But when the birds turn, hard raindrops fall from her
eyes, she hides
It under the bed, in the closet, on top of the
Shelf, in her head; she cries softly, watering the lilies, a
storm over the koi pond.

These are the secrets I cannot keep:
That if all the grains of sand would swap for her thoughts,
Children could play forever in her sandpit. Every touch
since my bloom was prophetic—
A summer's haze dares not to substitute her warmth
She is an eternal bud of light, uncovered by the blanket
of the sky
She is an everblooming tree, every step leaves a delicate
footprint where I can grow
Even the lilies come out for her laughter
I've discovered something in the dark
A silence pregnant with meaning,
It was no Greek that led me to the truth, but I know this;
She will love me through the mist and the dirt
That erodes my feet and the time I leave my nest,
I cry in her arms. She laughs, says "It's fiction, my dear"
Forgiveness at her fingertips
The night sky is empty, but in us, lies the blossom of

truth—
That it was her the magi had followed,
Sweet root of the cosmos: The theology of mothers,
And I am an heir to such divinities.

Model Aeroplanes

Susannah Hearn

My desk is a mess. I haven't been into work for three days and my books and laptop have been replaced by flattened sheets of newspaper and tiny plastic pots of acrylic paint.

The envelope that came in this morning's post is at the side of the desk, but I haven't opened it. I can't open it.

Instead, I pop open a pot of acrylic paint and lean over my model aeroplane in the harsh white light of my desk lamp. It's late — 00:12 — but building the model took all my time.

It's too soon to start painting yet, but I start anyway — maybe I want you to chide me. But you don't, not this time.

"Come on gramps," I mumble. "Tell me I'm doing it wrong. Tell me I have to give the glue longer to dry."

The newspaper crinkles as I lean forward. The air stinks of chemical paint.

I can't see you, but I know your arms are crossed — in that brown aviator jacket you never take off. Maybe you're looking to the skies now whilst I work on the model.

I dip my brush in the water.

You were always looking to the skies. Remember when I was a kid and you used to take me to your allotment on the weekends? I'd run through the bean poles, chasing butterflies and you'd tell me one day I too could fly.

Up there, child. Look to the skies.

But somehow, I never found the time. I'm twenty-five now, but still not a single flying lesson under my belt. Always too busy, never enough minutes to spare. So we made model aeroplanes instead. In snatches of time on Sunday afternoons when I wasn't working or shopping or working or sleeping.

Spitfires, bi-planes, boeing 747s, all lined up on shelves at the side of the room — perfectly glued, perfectly painted — next to the photo of us at the allotment. I'm distracted by a toy. You're looking to the skies.

I slick the first line of paint across our new model — a Felixstowe seaplane.

It's a poor replacement for flying, isn't it?

We almost made it. I booked the course a month ago. But then you fell ill. I thought you'd be fine. I thought we'd be opening the tickets together now, putting on matching jackets. I didn't realise your lungs were weak. Mum says you didn't want to burden me — I was so busy.

I rest my paintbrush in the pot of water. 04:03

You're still looking to the skies. But you can't help it now, can you?

I reach for the envelope. It's crisp and smooth, like hospital sheets. I should have found the time.

I could have found the time.

And even though I know it's too late now, that's why I send an email to my boss saying I quit. That's why I shrug on my aviator jacket and go to the airfield to meet my instructor. Our instructor.

We get into a Grob 120 TP Prefect — you and me

gramps — and the Earth falls away in blue-green sea and green-yellow fields until all that's left is sky.

I just wish we could have seen it together.

RELATIONSHIPS

Fragments

Alexia Oerter

The House

Your family had a beautiful home. The ceilings were high, the gardens were grand, and it was filled with paintings you couldn't touch and chairs you couldn't sit on. You used to wear those dresses that would float all around you when you spun. I remember you telling it all while we sat in front of our fireplace drinking black lemon tea — two sugars and a dash of milk. But all that didn't matter to you. Grandeur never mattered. The only thing you could not live without was the 21st of December, the shortest day of the year, and how the sun would start to set at exactly 4:38, and how the pink and orange light would travel through the tainted glass of the west wing windows in such a way as "to make the room breathe," you'd say. And just for that, there is nowhere else you would have rather lived.

The Goodbyes

Your father hugged you like he never had before. You felt the love and the desperation and the resignation, all together in one last tight embrace. You never saw him again, but you always said that at least you got to say goodbye. You told me you were holding on to that goodbye when he turned and walked away only glancing back once, when he climbed into his car, when you ran after it through the empty cloud of dust it left behind, when news arrived that he would not be coming back. I remember the spark in your eyes, a lens of sadness and resilience. It was my turn to take you in my arms. He was never scared you know; it was 1944, he did not have time to be scared.

The Party

I was invited by a friend, an old school friend, but gone were the knee-socks, the spilled ink, and the echoes of teachers' angry scoldings. "My father's associates will be there," he said. "You might end up making connections," he said. We had been done with school for a few years but we were still what society would call 'young men', and young men at these parties were children come to dress up as adults. I got in through the front door with him to a house filled with smoke, roaring music and masked decadence — the worst kind. His father introduced us to important men with tough handshakes and pretentious smiles never reaching eyes. One of them might even have been your husband, but I would not have known him. And in that sea of self-importance, there you were, sitting at the long dining table with the other wives. You were smoking a cigarette, drinking pink champagne and draped in fur, unaware of your own splendour. You were smiling, talking, listening with one ear, laughing as if paying real attention, but your wandering eyes travelled inwards to a world unknown to anyone but yourself. You were something else. You still are. Bathed in the light coming from the fireplace, you met my stare with one of your own, fearless, and I was yours.

Misfortune

People say you never forget your first love. And perhaps people make the mistake of believing that a first love is always a right one. But is it? Some first loves never grow when the lovers do, and some first loves grow old before the lovers do. Before you knew it, your husband was a stranger inhabiting familiar skin, a proud man, an anxious man, an old man. You were his, by law and by will until law became prison. You thought you couldn't leave. You couldn't possibly leave a son behind, alone and defenceless against possessiveness and harsh words. Until the son was diagnosed as worse than the father. You know it was not his fault, nor yours. It doesn't excuse anything, but it isn't really his fault. Even so, I do hope you never forget; I do hope you always feel fortunate to look back and see what you escaped from. When in doubt, look into my eyes, my angel, remember what you escaped for.

A Different Life

They warned you right away that a life with me would be a 'very different' one. They warned you that our age difference would be talked about with no rest. But you never cared. Of the two of us you were the youngest, not in age as we know well, but in your mind — a free-spirit burning with an independence refused to you for too long by your previous husband. A life with me meant hard work, and a small apartment, and bare walls, but you never complained, or resented leaving everything behind. You were always smiling, even when I felt like I was letting you down. You would lift my chin up so I could see that smile of yours. Until your natural faith in me and our hard work lead to bigger apartments and jewellery and art and abundance in every single aspect of our wonderful life. You were draped in fur again, a glass of pink champagne in hand and strings of pearls dangling from your perfect neck. It was a different life that's for sure, but at the end of the day it was us — simply us.

Reunion

We always knew you would leave before me. We were prepared and came the day when we stopped dreading it. You grew more and more tired and your sight got weaker and weaker with every passing day. Our goddaughter called the day before. I kissed you on the forehead as a farewell from her, do you remember? I took care of her you know. You would be so proud of me, my angel, and of the person she's growing up to become. Now, I am lying on an uncomfortable bed, in a cold hospital room. The walls are bare and an acrid smell hangs everywhere. I try to talk but nobody understands; I try to keep my eyes open but it's too hard. She was here though — I saw her, I think. She held my hand. When everybody leaves, I think of you, my angel, and your clear blue eyes that now see better than ever before. You look at me, greet me home again. It's the 21st of December, 4:38 in the afternoon, and the room breathes.

Winter's Kiss

Chloe England

Like a blanket, the leaves cover me. Red and green hues caress my face like lovers, their paper-sharp edges almost dangerous, threatening beauty. I am still, and I wait.

Winter comes all too quick, like a dog-bark. The snow falls gracelessly, whisked into a tornado by the ruthless wind. The drops of white diamond caress my face like enemies, frighteningly cold — fingers of the dead. I am still, and I wait.

You are frantic. Door-slam, feet-thump excited. You run to me, trailing the rose-petal sled behind you, thump meets tug. Under the dead leaves, eaten up by the cold, you are alive. You are electric. You are beautiful. You are the cosiness of a fireplace, the sweetness of hot chocolates on Sundays.

Face to face, we smile. Oh, how we have waited for the cold to warm us. Milky white teeth parade between strawberry lips, crooked and kind.

The sled fits two, barely. Sixteen means stringy limbs and awkward fits. I cling to your marshmallow coat, muted green, and think of blanket-leaves, of missing you. Christmas brings presents. My favourite? Your return.

Tableau of Terror and Travel

Carrie Nielson

Ripple, read the tear from my eye,
Enveloping a sigh,
Sat on my hands which couldn't say hi.

High as a kite, my one flew through,
Sinking a yacht, drove my body
Into the blue,

Blew me a kiss,
Broke my bed and body for you,
Yanking the yellow Sea,

See my hands trying to hold on,
And reach the remainders of you,

Rose Petal Jam

Ridhi Kotecha

05:20. My hand trembles as I slip a cigarette between my lips. I have to flick the spark wheel several times before it manages to ignite the tip. I inhale deeply, closing my eyes as the smoke rushes into my lungs. I trap it there, letting it reacquaint itself with my cells. Exhaling with a long sigh, I open my eyes and watch the smoke circle away into the clouds. It's been four months since I quit. Four months since I lost my husband. It's almost time to go inside and open up, but I still have time for another one, another breath of fresh air.

05:26. I always get here forty minutes before my staff arrive. I need that quiet time in the morning, alone. I need time to sharpen my knives and prepare myself for the unwelcome questions and publicity, the infamous "what is your secret ingredient?" Like a magician never reveals their magic trick, a chef never reveals their secret ingredient. I never used to have a 'secret ingredient,' not until a couple of months ago. I've been getting a lot of nosy interviewers asking me about my personal life ever since it was unveiled that my husband had gone missing and has now been presumed dead. They're so full of shit, acting like they care, giving me pity. They don't care. They just want some juice, something new to write about, another story to make headlines and dirty, dirty money. I hate reporters, they thrive off other people's misery. Everyone expected me to hit rock bottom when he went missing, but I didn't, I just kept going and I just got better. I even made the front page in a bunch of newspapers as 'Widow Turns Death Into Delicacies'. Then suddenly, everybody started asking me "what is your secret ingredient?" I never spilled the beans though; I've always been somewhat of a 'clean-freak'.

05:58. My staff should be arriving anytime soon. I've opened everything up, checked all the surfaces and ordered today's ingredients fresh from the market. I'm a vegetarian, I always have been; the idea of serving dead animals to people disgusts me - I'd rather serve human flesh. All of my restaurants serve vegetarian food, only.

06:00. My first member of staff has arrived, Rose. She's always the first one to come. She's a lot like me, much prettier though. We used to be close when my husband was around. We aren't anymore. My husband introduced us at a party at his house a couple of years ago, she used to cater a lot for his mother's parties. She was looking for a job back then and, coincidentally, I had just fired my sous-chef and gave her a chance at taking his spot — she was brilliant and has been with me ever since.

06:03. The other staff start trickling in now, heading straight towards the sink. It's like watching a line of ants hurry towards spilt honey. I detest dirty hands. I always tell my staff that they must have hands clean enough to perform an operation.

06:10. Everyone is ready at their stations. This time four months ago my husband was still in our bed, fast asleep. I would make fresh crêpes with jam for him every morning before I left for work. It was his favourite thing to eat. He only went to work around eight o'clock. By the time he'd come back, I'd be asleep. We open up for breakfast at seven o'clock. I start writing my newest creations, 'The Specials,' up on the board. Savouries: Blackberry Brie Omelette, Basque Potato and Camembert Frittata, Baked Egg Danish with Kimchi and Spinach. Sweets: Brioche French Toast with Vanilla-Bean Ice Cream, Chilled Blueberry Soup, Coconut Cream Muffins. I love creating new and weird dishes, throwing in the unexpected ingredient, not sticking to the recipe — I cook like I live my life. Well, at least like I used to live my life. Everything has changed now, ever since he disappeared. I feel guilty, all the time. But at least my cooking got better, I mean, ever since I got back in the kitchen after you know… I became a star. A sensation. I have my own 'special' freezer now, in my office, no one has access to it except me. It's where I keep my stash for 'The Specials'… my secret ingredient.

10:50. The last customers should be leaving around now, we open-up again at one o'clock for lunch. I normally stay at the restaurant till then, I never used to go home for lunch, it's not like I'd have anyone to eat with anyways. Rose would always leave for lunch though. She doesn't anymore, not since the past couple of months. It's always just the two of us now, lingering behind. She doesn't speak to me, and if we happen to make eye contact, she darts her eyes elsewhere. She seems nervous around me nowadays.

11:47. I step outside for a smoke. I take a long drag,

holding it in my lungs. I don't have any children. My husband and I, we never really wanted our own kids. Maybe he did? I puff out the smoke, watching the it fade away. I take another drag, feeling the nicotine enter my bloodstream. I think he fell out of love with me, long before he disappeared. I think — he was seeing someone else. I force out the smoke, my chest grows heavy. I take one last drag, feeling the heat of the tip burning the skin of my fingers. I can't stop seeing his face now. My hands around his neck — I can see into his soul through his eyes, all the lies... her face. I can see everything clearly now. I exhale slowly, liberating my lungs of the sickening smoke. I think I'm going to quit again.

11:53. I go back inside. I call for Rose. I tell her I want her to get something for me from my freezer. She looks shocked, confused. I give her my keys and tell her that I'm retiring my post. That I want her to take over now, I want to entrust her with my secret ingredient, so that she too can use it. But only on the condition: she swears never to share it with another soul. I tell her to fetch me a bag, right from the bottom of the freezer. She nods quietly, takes the keys and walks over to my office. About a half a minute later, I hear a scream, and then a thud.

05:20. I start to open up as usual, prepare for the new day. No smokes for me anymore, I quit yesterday.

06:02. My staff are starting to arrive now and are setting-up their stations. I head over to my freezer. I open the lid and push some bags of frozen vegetables to one side. There it is, my secret ingredient. I've almost used all of it up in these past few months, but that's okay, I restocked yesterday. I push a couple of bags to the other side, and there it is, my new secret ingredient. I don't think they would taste good together though, I don't think the flavours would match. Maybe, I'll just use them separately, individually — how they're meant to be used. I decide to use the new secret ingredient today, in remembrance of my husband and decide to have only that on 'The Specials'. I'll make his favourite, and I'm sure if he were here, he would love it. Especially with my new secret ingredient. Although, I'm sure he's already familiar with the taste.

06:53. I head back into the kitchen to write on 'The Specials' board, my newest creation: Crêpes with Rose Petal Jam.

Old Age Surprise

Chloe Jaques

She was an old lady,
a wad of history and aphorisms,
not like us, not angry, not restless.
A sweet sag in pink felt,
with slippers and slippers and slippers
and crochet blankets,
and an ornamental frog
of substantial diameter.
One phone call,
she joked about using it
as a weapon.
She liked grey cats,
and Northcote park,
and the day next door's boy
took his earring out for good.
She would stir only sometimes,
like a rustle, and mostly stayed
inside, to hum.
We were surprised to find
upon her death
the corpse of her husband
out on the patio,
wrapped in several tarpaulins
to mask the smell of skin and rot.

Hi Darling, Just Calling to Say

Daniella Clarke

Hi Darling, Just Calling to Say I've been thinking an awful
lot lately
About all the things you'd do that rubbed me
The wrong way:
How it was always your goddamned music
In the car and after dinner.
There's only so many times
You can listen to Levon by Elton
Without losing the will.
You were messy — you'd always wait for me to
Change the sheets, feed the cat, turn the
lights off downstairs.
Don't even get me started on that godawful
night
When you vomited all over yourself
At your friend Joan's house.
One minute you were singing
And the next you were clinging to her with
one hand
And her toilet seat with the other,
Decorating the tiled floor with the pasta you'd
had earlier
And the two bottles of white wine you'd drunk.
You always wanted to seem sophisticated
Because you could say
'Châteauneuf-du-Pape'.
Well, good for you.

I always hated,
How you would run a bath and then complain
When the water got cold and I'd say
Well, you shouldn't have left it so long
And you would shout and shout and shout at
me,
Call me a bastard—
And well, after a while of thinking of all the
ways
You bothered me, I started wishing
That you would come back
And bother me again soon.

Fire, Ice

Sophie Wellington

Slippery connections,
A fragile rope of ice.
I'm afraid I have been selfish,
Kept too tight a grip on you, an individual.

True statements.
My eyes rest on red herrings—
Subtle crimson flashes
Catch my attention.

I do not mind being a snake of downpour.
I do not mind being blue.

INJUSTICE

Deep Throat

Lumba Phiri

This poem is about how I learnt to swallow. How I forced my throat to break the confines of science. How I raised my tired middle finger to biology and morphed into a hybrid of myself. It is about the thick, murky liquid, about its alkaline burning a path through my body. It is about the sensation of thousands of years of oppression absorbing into my skin, marking my cells as their own. It is about the tribal drums beating their loud noise through my oesophagus and barraging through the barriers my mother's body oh so lovingly gave to me.

It is about forgetting my worth, about considering only 'peace'. This poem is about how I learnt to swallow. How I learnt to deep throat their racism, how I let them thrust their ignorance further into me and abandoned my gag reflex. This is about submission, about learning my place, about suspending my need for respect, my need for a home, for a sanctuary. It is the story of how I gained a new-found reverence for those that came before me. How I learnt that 'yes sir' can take many different forms, that my showy laugh, my silence in the midst of my persecution, my acceptance of their new names for my name. My refusal to inform them that when my mother called me by my name in thanks to God she did not mean for you to one day stand before me and spit on her sacrifice, she did not mean for you to see her laid half open before you, vulnerable, strong, god and think it okay to rob her of her offering. My name, a prayer to the most-high, a proclamation of greatness, of the goodness of a God so mighty he took me from and brought me into this world all at the same time. This is about the scar I carry every day, about my neck cut open, about my mother pouring herself into me as I took my first laboured breaths as if to say here, all I have I give to you even as you desert me, even as you leave me scared, open, in agony. This scar I wear upon my neck as a reminder that even as I came into this world beating my loud arrogant noise, it fought to drag me back down into the pits of extinction. This scar so quietly powerful it twitches as I bear my teeth and smile back at your degrading humour, this scar so telling it fights to disappear ashamed of the person I have come to be. This scar threatening to burst open once more and pull the life from me rather than feel every contraction as I mould myself anew to accommodate you; as I learn to swallow the words you ejaculate with such blatant disregard.

This poem is about the first time you said Nigger. About how I watched the word fall into the sink I was washing dishes in and my back grew weary from the weight of carrying my ancestors' sacrifice, my back crackled as the progress you boast so proudly of trickled down the drain tangled in pieces of decomposing cheese. It is about the second time you said Nigger and my drunken stupor turned to cold focus, about how I straightened my back and cleared my throat of all that Nigger you thought you heard. How I positioned myself so that you would see me, not cotton picking, back door using, uniform-wearing Nigger but me, me who laughed when you called me by your names, me who chastised you for using the word Nigger like you would tell the sky to stop pouring down rain, powerless, inferior, awe-struck. It is about the third time you said Nigger and I pondered what they fought for, I pondered how Kenneth Kaunda bought a bike through a window, I pondered the jobs we never got, the huge corporations that waltz into our Zambia and dared not hire one of us to run their companies, I pondered the thousands of acres of our land they own, I pondered the 90% unemployment as compared to the number of trucks filled with copper driving merrily out of our borders, how they syphon the resources from our land, how they leave us their cancers, their sperm, their pollution, their shit and take our royalty, take our magic and sell it back to us. It is about the fourth time you said Nigger, and the fifth and the sixth time, you motherfucker. It's about how my face became gradually less willing to construe itself into a pleasant expression. It is about the way my whole body contracts as I call on Jesus and ask him to stop me. It's about a rage that comes from the pits of the millions of starving children.

This poem is about how I learnt to swallow, about how I filled myself with you, with your thick murky liquid, with your racism and your names for my name that steal the glory embedded in me, deeper that your condescending tone could touch. It is about how I allowed you to reshape my refuge, how I accommodated you so completely that there was no room for myself, there was no room for the sacrifice made for me, no room for my mother who tore herself open for me.

You say Nigger and I watch from the corner of a room I do not recognise as a fire so lit rises from the floor, closes

in from within the walls, seeps in from the ceiling and
envelops your rancid, misogynistic, racist existence and
vanishes.

Ashes

Melissa Oram

Reach around with an iron fist, strangle land and sea at
whim.
Again, and again, and again.
Surveying eyes glint like gold
And ears hear only the whispers of wealth
Echoing across continents.
Pull up your charters and your maps and your compass
Point fingers at people and places
Calling them your own.
Again, and again, and again.
Rise from your self-made ruin
Sail with your back turned
And accept the pats on the shoulder
And the exchange of blood-money.
Move on with your life.
As if nothing happened.
Pass on the Island Stories
With as much ease as you passed on people
To sons who not only forget
But bathe in the tainted waters of old.
Disguised as glittering cascades
Legacies printed in bold words
Behind which hide the people relegated to distasteful
past.
Not to be recalled.
The flag hoisted again, and again, and again.
Red, unhinged passion turned to blood by the blue waters

which transported sadistic ideas, and stamped a white
hand on newly found sand.
Built behind our greatness lies centuries of subjugation in
the name of Britannia,
Swept into the abyss of the past,
Ash in the haunted graveyard of history.

Island Secrets

Jude Flashman

Bumping along dirt tracks—
Sweet faces standing by corrugated homes, watching.
Luscious green palms swaying high above heads—
On the ground, dust pervades.

Winding further in—
Sanitised estates and gates left far behind.
The dirt track reveals the islanders' secrets
Creeping into the voyeur's mind, awareness of Western
Sin.

Sparkling clear water—
Thwacking sounds, voices unite in song and laughter.
Children meander, women wash—
Unceasing slapping of fabric on rocks.

Discomfort and dismay expressed to the guide.
He turns with some distaste,
We pity you, imprisoned alone in your cell, feeding
insatiable machines.
No wonder your women's brains are unwell.

Waves

Claudia Kelley

The deep blue August sky descended over the beach, washing itself out into a pale watercolour just above the sea. Gulls wheeled through the twilight, beaks flashing. Their shrieks had settled from a mid-day frenzy into a wail muffled by the rushing waves. As they swept through the air, one landed with a soft thud on something just above the reaches of the purple-grey foam. The tide inched higher, hissing as it caught the edges of the object. The gull moodily thrust its head at a long black strap that floated back and forth like seaweed through the foam.

Just as the object began to tip under the weight of a wave, a blur of limbs darted down the beach, breaking through the wave to grab the bag. It streamed water as it swung from the boy's shoulder, and beat against his hip as he strode back across the beach. The glow at the horizon was now faltering. A thin sand path wove up a craggy hill tufted with grass and pocked with rocks and rabbit holes. He scrambled up the hillside and broke through the undergrowth into the parking lot.

It had begun to rain. The drizzle made a halo out of the single streetlamp. The boy suddenly lurched forward over the bag, a sob bursting from his body and rattling around the parking lot. He sucked in cold air, steadied himself. He unzipped the bag and gazed at the contents: a sandy pair of trainers; a pale, bloated copy of *The Waves*; a bag of Tangfastics. As always.

*

"What kept you?" his mother asked, lifting her head from her newspaper. She studied her son from across the room. Bedraggled as he was, he was beautiful, with blue-green eyes and dark curling hair, as if he had sprung fully formed from the sea. The children, she thought wryly, were the one thing she and their father had cooperated on.

"Sorry. Forgot my bag." He swung an arm around her shoulder and kissed her on the cheek. She smiled, appeased.

"Right, well — fine. Get it out of here, you're dripping all over the floor," she said, gesturing at the growing puddle.

"Honestly Max," she mused, after a pause, "this must be the fifteenth time you've done that."

"Third, actually," he mouthed. She didn't hear.

"It's a good job it's not been washed away yet."

*

Max hung the bag to dry, then climbed the two flights of stairs to his bedroom. When they had left London (and Max's father) for Dorset ten years ago, the prospect of an attic room was all that could brighten Max's seven-year-old attitude. Propping the trainers by the radiator, he laid the packet of sweets and the book on his desk. The yellow Tangfastics bear grinned up at him. Again he felt that sudden welling in his chest and throat, a wave ready to consume him. Exhaling sharply, he threw himself onto his bed and lay face-up, scanning the wall. It was covered with race numbers from countless cross-country events. The familiarity calmed him, though a dull ache remained in his chest, and he turned his head to look once again at the objects on his desk. He would return them tomorrow.

*

When Max awoke the next morning his room was that pale golden colour that promises a rare cloudless summer day. He felt for his phone — it read 07:47, Saturday 8 August. He'd taken to waking up early in the holidays, and today of all days was not one to wallow in bed. He dressed quickly and slipped down the stairs, past his snoring brothers' rooms.

"Tea, Max?" his mother asked, her back to the kitchen door.

"Cheers. Normal is good," he answered. He swung open the fridge door and plucked out a silver takeaway carton.

"Sleep alright?" She set the mug in his spot at the kitchen table. He pursed his lips, formed the words *Yeah, fine*, and shook his head.

"Not great, actually." His mother stopped suddenly and looked at him.

"It's today, isn't it. Oh, sweetheart, I'm so sorry." She took the container from his hands, placed it on the table, and hugged him tightly. He leaned his forehead against her shoulder, as if he wasn't nearly a foot taller.

"Thanks, ma," he mumbled. He smiled weakly. "Time for breakfast I think."

*

The Huxleys' house was ten minutes by bike. The two families were very close, and he knew the house like his own. He left his bike in the driveway, hitched the bag higher on his shoulder, and peered through the backdoor, which stood open to the sun.

"Anyone home?" Max called, stepping into the kitchen.

"Max!" Mrs Huxley appeared, smoothing her frizzy

hair. It seemed like someone had crackled electricity through her.

"I just thought I'd pop by to see you and Lucy," he said. Mrs Huxley nodded, sighing heavily.

"Thanks, Max. She's in her room."

Max hesitated outside Lucy's room, glancing down the hallway at a closed door with PERCY across the front in painted wooden letters.

"Lucy, can I come in? It's Max." He heard rustling, the sound of eight-year-old feet on the carpet, the lock turning in the door, the feet padding away again. He opened it gently and stepped into her room. Sunlight filtered through the cartoon seascape of the drawn curtains, tinting the room an underwater blue. Lucy said nothing, just watched him from her nest of blankets. He sat on the edge of her bed and pulled the bag onto his lap. Her eyes widened.

"No! It's for him!" Lucy's bottom lip quivered dangerously.

"I know, but he would want you to keep it to remember him better.'

"But it's his stuff! He needs to have it."

"Lucy —"

"How is he going to run, or read, or eat any sweets where he is?" she asked desperately.

"I'm sure he has everything he needs. Look, I know it's hard, but he'd be sharing these sweets with us anyway. And he'd want you to read this." Lucy gave a watery smile.

"I just miss him. When can I see him?" she whispered.

"I know." Max stroked her blonde hair. He missed Percy too - his best friend, the first person he had met when they'd moved from London, with whom he'd shared divorcing parents and cross-country running. Who had drowned three years ago today. "We'll see him one day, I promise."

*

Stepping into the blinding warmth of the day, Max felt a tremendous weight lifting from him. He'd left Lucy in a slightly better state than he had found her: at least now her door was unlocked. He breathed deeply as he cycled home, exhaling out as much pent-up grief as he could. It had been a draining morning. He arrived home with his mind clearer than it had been for a while. Perhaps it was comforting Lucy that had been so therapeutic. He resolved to spend the rest of the day doing absolutely nothing.

*

Later that day he lay sprawled on his stomach in the garden reading his book, his shadow lengthening across the grass in front of him. He heard the landline ringing through the open door of the house and got up to answer it.

"Hello?" he said, balancing the phone on his shoulder. He wandered absently through to the kitchen, holding his book open between the fingers of his left hand, and reached for the fridge door with the right.

"Oh, hi there Max, have you got Lucy with you?" It was Mrs Huxley.

"No, she's not at ours. Why d'you ask?"

"She's out of her room, thank God, but she said she was going to see someone and hasn't come back. Oh well — I'm sure she'll be back soon. Thanks Max!" Mrs Huxley chattered.

Max's mouth went dry. "Oh my God," was all he

managed, as he dropped the phone.

He was at the parking lot in minutes. His bike clattered to the tarmac as he tore down the path towards the beach. He skidded to a halt atop the cliff, wildly scanning the sand. A few clusters of rainbow towels, the odd umbrella, but no sign of her bright blonde hair among the few placid beachgoers. Holding his breath, he lifted his eyes to the edge of the sea. A cold shock jolted through his body. How could nobody have noticed? He bellowed Lucy's name. Just about where the bag had been yesterday, something floated back and forth like seaweed on the surface of the waves.

Begum

George Ford

One step forward two steps back Three bodies lay bloody
on an open track One had a gram, one had a knife
Reason enough to take a life Two steps forward three
steps back The groomed girl's baby fades to black How
can I be judged for what I said when I was 15? You'll ask
in your future trial They shoved it in your face you'll say
You'll still regret nothing to this day Because what is
sacrifice Getting nothing for paying a price Why would
you choose to sacrifice your greed? Shed your excess
to those crying out in need Sitting in a house worth a
million
meals Ignoring the humility of a man who kneels Left out
by the process, left out in the rain Let me have another
chance, let me start again No. No excuses. No second
chances. No reruns. No Empathy. Rags to riches, riches
to riches. Success is a drug and society's addicted Now
spin the wheel, hold on tight Pray you end up with a life,
not a fight.

Giving Up

Harry Caton

"stammer: to make involuntary stops and repetitions in speaking"

I'll wonder why you find it so tiresome—
my stops, sticking, and stammer.

It isn't the movement, locked in my mouth
like some gobstopper, oversized, glottal;

nor the seconds, stretched through
minutes, caught in an unwound clock.

No — it's those little glances, that space
of the moment, the clutch of some frigid smile:

you'll quaver, blink, look away—
look back, look bored, and sigh—

check watch when you think I can't see,
even loose a quick smirk for the nerves.

And your eyes betray you, flicking away
before they can even connect;

your patience held as only a front,
framing some meek amends.

I'll also find it exhausting—

but you're the one to give up.

Stained Cloth

Erica Barnes

*Many peat bog bodies found from the Iron Age are thought to
be victims of human sacrifice. These include bodies of members of
the Suebi tribes found in southern Germany. Suebi priests would
tour with a cart draped in cloth, dedicated to the fertility goddess
Nerthus. The cart blessed those it visited, and is said would
prevent war, but when its journey was over the slaves used to clean
it were sacrificially drowned in lakes, which became bogs.*

*

The earth is pregnant. The lumps and bumps of
ancient peat bogs are fertile, fresh with moss and hard
grasses, and far away from where civilisation has carved
at the peat for fuel. There are no men here with trucks
and bags. There are no fatty parcels of mud stacked up,
or clean-cut canals in the ground. Plants have been
allowed to take root and spatter over the plains: heather,
grasses, and even the suggestions of forests. There's a
forest just south of nowhere, where the evergreens are so
old their roots are as thick as my thighs. These roots
rummage down the slope of the earth, into the wet foul
stink of a pool. A small lake, technically, but nobody
expects lakes to smell so sour.

This is where I live. This is where I was buried.

I lost my thumbnail digging myself out the earth. This
was years ago. My cuticles are loose; so is my hair, my
teeth, my deflated skin. Still, often I kneel and bury my

hands in the muck to remember what it felt like — cold slick under your fingers, dead roots tied around your knuckles, and the primal urge to stretch and burrow that lasts long after your muscles have atrophied. Every time I unearth my hands I have to count my nails again.

My hands are now thin, like the rest of me. My calluses are gone, lost under the folds of my leathered skin. The last thing I ever did was scrub cloth with these hands; now it's my skin that creases beneath my knuckles. These fingertips have long forgotten the cut of the reeds we used to cleanse Nerthus' cart. When I first scrambled out of my grave, grasses pierced my leg and cut away at what precious skin I had left. When I think back, I hope dying didn't hurt like that. Even after all this time I have to think the goddess wouldn't want that for me. It's hard enough she wanted me dead.

I've overheard people speaking, recalling what I presume are stories. It doesn't happen often — there's no safe path to walk. The peat is unsteady and the mounds slough apart; rabbits burrow deep pits and traps. I feel the earth's unrest beneath my feet and in my bones and I wonder if it's what woke me. When I do hear their stories, they're in strange, bastardised tongues. I've stopped trying to listen. Instead, I sit in my lake and tell my own story to the frogs and the worms.

I always start with the feel of wood. This is something all of us in the bog know, sheltered as we are by our family of trees. I explain to the dragon flies that carved wood has been skinned off the bark they slot their needle legs in. It is stripped away by sharpened flint, chopped into pieces, and slotted together. Then I usually have to explain what flint is, and what anyone would want to make out of wood when trees are so helpful as they are.

We usually get side-tracked. Eventually, I get to talk about Nerthus' cart.

The cart is often in my dreams. Its wooden skeleton was just a host for magnificent wheels, round and fertile with spires and offshoots. Then, tied in knots and weaved amongst the spindles, was the fabric I cared for. The priests had complied the wool of fifteen, maybe twenty sheep — my father was a shepherd, but I never learnt to count. There were banners of sickly red, so strong I worried the yellow and the blue strips would embarrassed. I recall running my nails (strong, back then) over the knitted divots and following the zigzags of colour. The people didn't get to touch the cart when it visited the farms; only the privileged and the dead had that right. From our master's land we watched it arrive — my brother and I, with our backs bent, spying the haughty necks of the priests as we tilled the earth.

This earth was barren. Empty, over farmed — the people blamed us, of course, and our lowly hands. My brother cursed the cows that grazed there. Our cows were not like the ones that pulled the cart. Nerthus' heifers shone — ours were scraggly, half-starved things with dull coats and gnarled horns. He swore at them, spat at them, and watched in pointed silence as they pummelled the crops with their oblivious hooves. I turned to Nerthus. While he was beaten for his smart mouth, I curled myself up in the hay and I prayed. I prayed so hard my joints would crack, the force of it so strong that it felt like roots had sprouted from my body. Behind my eyelids, stars grew into the robust figure of a woman. The indents of my hands over my eyes became blooming thighs the shape of ears of wheat; the little rags that hid my body became motherly swathes. The pods of the trodden grains became teeth to me. The curved stalks became proud smiles. When the priests came to the family to ask for slaves to wash Her cart, I felt the seedlings move beneath my feet.

(At this point of my story I'll have bored off the dragonflies, but the toads will have stayed. Last spring a family of tadpoles moved into the pool in the dip of my clavicle so they could feel my throat move.)

They walked us to the lake in silence. My brother and a woman from the next farm over were tasked with untethering the heifers from the cart — he eyed their hooves and rubbed his scars. The priests then brought the rest of us over to the water and had us undress the wood. Together we stroked at the fabric, picking at knots, lingering at the oak to feel it dampen as it began to rain. Raindrops blossomed on my neck, dripped down the grooves of my fleshy cheek and past my lips. We breathed the fresh scent of rainfall and clean water on reeds. When droplets slapped the surface of the lake, the water rebounded and gave off a cloud of white watery spores. The air was alive with it — I was alive with it. The sting of water in my eyes meant nothing when I was inhaling the breath of Nerthus.

I basked in the connection. She'd heard me — of course she had. Now the rain would replenish our soil and my brother would not be beaten. I was blind to the waterlogged fields and suffocating crops; when the hurried priests ordered us to wash the cloth I scrubbed the hardest. I remember the black peat stains, the brown smears, the hoof shaped tears. I remember my fingers bleeding but not the feeling of having blood. I remember the hands on my head, knuckles digging at my back, the familiar screamed swears of my brother. I remember being pushed underwater, but not what it felt like to drown.

The frogs don't understand what drowning is. I slip into the bog to make bubbles with my nose to show them. These bubbles are playful; they float on the water's skin lazily until popped by an anxious pond-skater. My final bubbles in life were lazy too, in a way. The struggle didn't last long; the little grain in my stomach only made for a few kicks' worth of energy. It's hard to know who to fight when caught in a net of darkness — it's hard to move your feet when reeds and lily stalks have cuffed them. The taste was foul, brackish and obscenely salty, so I shut my mouth in the first few seconds. People like me had learnt not to bother screaming, anyway.

I'd never been afraid of the dark. My brother was — though he wouldn't admit it. He clung to torchlight, but I would always be left to watch our cattle at night. This wasn't the same darkness. My body was entrenched in flat brown. The shapes lost definition, becoming smears that radiated a kind of sickness; patches of queasy green swam an indeterminate distance from my eyes. The blackness began at the edges of my vision and narrowed, squeezed alongside my lungs. Trampled, even. The last thing I saw was Nerthus' cloth floating towards me like a cascade of long hair, beautiful and potent and stained with my blood.

The creatures of the bog want to know about my brother; if he made it, or if he's here beneath us. They ask about the heifers and how soft their eyes were, if they were bathed and scrubbed and taken care of. Still, I can only regale what I know. I know the long climb of my consciousness out of the earth and the first jolt of my waking muscles. My diaphragm, flattened by decades of packing of mud, blossomed and inflated. My expansion cracked the pond bed. My hands sprouted through its crust like wheat stalks. Then my head, carefully eased through the wet. My brain had long since dried to lavender sticks and now my head drifts in the wind too easily, too fragile. I took one long, chattering death cough, and vomited the black ooze and frogspawn out of my lungs. And then I sat and waited for the oats to grow.

The Goodbye

Sophie Blake

Evening light seeps through the leaves
of a drowsy willow, whose arms encircle our little boat.
I lie, my body driftwood upon the water,
lulled into submission by the rhythm of the waves
which brush and breathe against the deck below.

The air is clear, the wind stable with a hint
of late spring fragrance, sprung from lilac fields
somewhere beyond. Wildflowers on the bank
beckon forth a summertime subtlety of colour,
pinpricks of poppy among a stitching of sapphire,
blending into a patchwork sky with cotton clouds.

We set out in the morning,
when the dawn bird foretold the day ahead,
and the night yielded to waking skies. This boat,
which sailed these waters every sepia summer,
shed a tear as we passed each crying brook,
but smiled in the light of the new sun.

My sister now sits at one end, a diary in her lap,
open at a eulogy, from which childhood
laments its departure. The pages are creased,
their flesh wizened and matured with memories.

She cannot see me, my hand reaching for hers,
nor hear my voice, now a flicker of debris on the breeze.

She cannot touch me nor feel my presence; instead, she
watches the sun fall, whispers prayers to the parchment,
then
looks ahead to the horizon. *I'm here,* I say. The evening
crow mourns.
Our eyes meet, and the goodbye is spoken.

Wreath

Zebulun O'Regan

She had buried time capsules:
vegetables that never took root;
photos — smoked blue from being
in the sun; keys to unknown locks;
dead fish; notes in bottles. Debris
swelled through the soil, her trowel
drew hieroglyphs on the ground.
She rolled up her moth-eaten sleeves,
their earthy smell — like tea leaves—
flushing from her clothes into her throat.

When she died, there was no one to
bury her — her spade lay lost at the bottom
of the garden, still caked with dirt.
She lay in the vegetable patch, vines coiling
around her neck, curling
through her hair.
Then the storm came—
sun whispering rainbows to the rain—
when the mud tossed itself up,
and her belongings clawed to the surface.
Magpies stole the keys;
puddles drowned the photos;
cats snatched the tin-foil fish,
soil bubbling, pulsing until the
Earth swallowed her whole,
as though she'd never existed at all.

SUFFERING

Empty Wrapper

Sam Bovey

Soft worms watch from below
As I toil
Spraying dirt overhead.
In the lunar spotlight
A wrapper,
Empty, stirs me to sweat.

Lifting it I choke
Empty fear rises like steam.
The shovel heavier,
With thoughts that compound,
Soft worms are watching still
In delight;
I return to that day in my mind:

"A ragged man forced it
(Silver skin, that scent)
Into my hands to eat
(Chocolate, that kept)
He laughed when I cried
(Sweet treat I repent!)
And the sky spun around, around,
And the sky spun around, around
The sky it spun around
I woke up in a hospital bed!"

I drop the shovel,

Kicking the wrapper
Alone and lingering by
Souls, whose scent is foul
I cry again
(They laughed)
At memory gone by,
And kick the wrapper in the ground
Upon the coffin's empty face.

Grief

Lauren O'Broin

It kicked me in the teeth,
And I felt my brain bounce
In the calcium cage coated
By my knotted hair.

It didn't hit me while I was down,
Instead watched the crimson smile that
Grew on my face as I littered the
Ground with yellowed pearls.

It spoon-fed me servings of acid,
Disguised in Avent Anti Colic bottles,
Pinching my nose until I swallowed.
But I couldn't keep it down.

I couldn't digest what it gave me,
It hurt too much.
And sometimes I feel it bubbling.

Disintegrating Ode for a Nightingale

George Richards

A blizzard   a figure inside it   I mistook it for a
nightingale
mistaking the blows for a cage   when they took out
the heart
it was boneless   a purple moon worn down to the
arterial
source we wrapped in burlap   years before I was
mistaking
fireflies & moths for my natural glow   I pulled them
in
for a tighter orbit   twisted into Lethe's tight knot of
root
& drooped my head among his flowers   I dropped
matches
into Jupiter just to watch a thick ball of hydrogen go
ablaze   asked
that when I died my ashes be danced in like a dark
confetti   now
I mistake nothing   the moon pulls the water to the
shore   a blue
mist drags the lake   the beady-eyed face in the
bathroom with
the evils is obviously your own but what exactly made it
yours you can't
remember   of Lincoln it is said that his melancholy
dripped
as he walked   Siddhartha is said to have been fine

before   his   melancholy   dripped   before   he   was
enlightened   his father hid
a kingdomful of corpses   but suffering is hard to
hide
when I gaze into the blizzard I mistake a nightingale for
a boy   smoke drips
from the leaves   the air he breathes is blue   he
doesn't notice
when I call   coughing blood onto the snow   his
heart aches

COAX

Mubanga Mweemba

These tidings wash me up to your shore.
I am the bottle and the message
and the messenger. Who flung
that empty Chardonnay from the east
to the edges of an unnamed coast.
You rub my spine as I hack up saltwater
steady in these episodes of nausea as I sway
and rock and tarry in disorientation.
When I can't see you hold me till I can.
When I can't talk you read to me
till I find language tolerable again.
When I get tired, you let me sleep
and you promise to wake me up.
Every time I recoil you keep an eye out for me
still seen from astronomical distances.
You always coax me back home

Mama Won't You See Me

Jake McDonald

And beneath blue pines, three mothers doze,
as fireflies float over a darkening knoll,
this cooing brook and these mirrored skies,
this great black head in stars baptised.
Wading in waterlilies, children silhouetted,
beaten musketeers of a miscarried day,
their algae-filled boots treading waves,
while perch wink from their coral caves.
Hear this girl as she moans in the gloom,
and leaves the tall reeds and these two boys,
scrambling the riverbank with eyes of water,
to mama who sleeps far from her daughter.
Note her throat now inked with bruises,
as fistfuls of lavender, stinking, as pooling
dark on white plastic; the boys end their game
as her finger soars in blame.
First boy, beady-eyed and lonely on the pale
tide, since coloured noon till moon's bony
light, knifed the pond for life, plucked scales
as if she-loves-me-nots. He wails.

Second boy, oyster-lipped with eyelids red,
sailed fields for anemone flowers now
spinning downstream, girl denied at the stile
so here he sighs. Then nosedives.
Hear this girl as she moans in the gloom,
and moans across this sequined night,

hiding her hands, bloody, to blame,
from mama who dreams and dreams quite alone,
in the sterile bleach of her
mobile phone.

I don't want you to fix me

Anonymous

Every time I have to explain this part of my life, I begin with the assurance that I am okay and I have moved on and you shouldn't worry.

In part, it is because I cannot bear to bring emotion into the description. Being watched with eyes full of pity is consuming and reminds me that I am the all-dreaded word; a 'victim'.

It is also partly because I don't want to be seen as a charity project for people to 'fix'. There is no advice required from my situation and so there is nothing that can be said to 'fix' it. People naturally always want to fix it. But I don't want to be broken and so the easiest way not to be is by refusing to be fixed.

But mostly, it is because there will always be a part of me that is worried you won't believe me. I won't cry when I tell you, so are you going to think it never really happened? Because surely if it happened I would be emotionally damaged, right? I might mention it simply in passing, as part of a larger less distressing story, and if I haven't deemed it worthy of an in-depth conversation then have I even endured this trauma? I might describe every instance of the night, in excruciatingly explicit detail, is that too cold for it to be real? It wasn't how you imagined these things to happen, it seems closer to regret, no? Surely, I should be choking on the very words, feeling too sick to express them? I might not be able to explain how it happened and, well, if I don't provide a story, it seems like a flawed accusation?

It isn't personal. It isn't you. It is the world. It is the person I trusted who laughed in my face as I shared and cried and shouted. It is my own damn confusion. How can this be real? I don't want it to be real. It cannot be my reality. I cannot be the one who was hurt in this way. Every fibre of my being is rejecting any flake of acceptance that this happened. And yet it did. And there is no changing that.

Everyone talks about what you can learn from bad situations, and sure, I learned from this. I learned how to have my power stripped away as I fought, begged, pleaded for it to return. I learned that sometimes, people can take from me, and I learned that sometimes, I cannot stop them. I learned that the people I seek sanctuary in can hurt me even when I think it isn't possible to hurt any more than I already am. I learned how to get up every day and fake a smile and fake a laugh. I learned how to pretend that I am not hollow now. I learned how to be helpless and I learned how to stay helpless every day since. I learned to live with anger. I learned that anger made its home inside of me and I keep it there, hoping it will guard away anyone who has the capacity to hurt me, which right now feels like everyone. But I did not learn how to heal. I don't know how to heal. All I know is anger now.

But anger isn't pretty or polite. It doesn't make me desirable. It makes me a problem. Maybe that's why people keep thinking I need fixing. Maybe they don't see a broken girl, maybe they see a problem. I have become inconvenient because of what somebody did to me, and because of what somebody said about it. But how dare you deem me a problem. How dare you dismiss the agony

I endure every single moment while you sit in your untarnished dome of safety, your amnesty from this pain, while I lay in the shattered remains of my innocence, cradling the bullet hole he tore inside me when he took away my autonomy.

Beehive

Clementine Venn

These hands are not his hands,
they are my hands.
But sometimes in my mind they are his hands,
and other times they are not hands at all,
they are claws.
That crawl their way between the cracks of my skin,
scooping out the love and leaving behind the shame.
I do not need protection from a man,
it is a man who I need protection from,
the only hands that hold me through the night are my
own.
And as I sink into the darkest corners of my mind,
I gain comfort in the sensation of my hair clinging to my
damp cheeks.
Tears are old friends that visit me at times like these,
when the monsters under my bed,
stop playing hide and seek.

His hands were greedy.
Once I had offered the treasures that are required for a
man to feel satisfied and
only then I would have peace of mind. In order to
survive I would conjure up spectacular stories:
one contained a lion who was addicted to honey. And so,
he ventured determinedly through endless acres of
woodland,
destroying every beehive, he could find.

But no amount of honey could fill his needs.
And so, eventually he died.

You are the lion,
and that night your fingers were searching for honey.
But instead of honey I began to bleed.
Perhaps, you assumed it was my first time.
You were not right.

A woman holds the sweetest honey between her thighs,
honey that no thief has the privilege to try.
You were a thief,
you stole my voice and my choice that night.
Took all my hopes and childhood dreams,
crammed them into the pores of my skin and sewed them
into the seams of my knickers.
You grew like bacteria in all the impure parts of me.

I scrubbed my body till it bled again.
Every meal I ate, I vomited out.
I wore oversized clothes, and spent most of my days
under the sheets,
but my palms still carried the sweat, whilst my feet
struggled to carry me.

I did everything I could to detox you out. But my body
jerks and clenches in the night, my hands grasping,
mouth gasping for air.
These hands,
the ones that carved out your name hundreds of times on
my thighs,
were also the hands that taught me the meaning of
pleasure on sleepless nights.

These hands,
spent what felt like an eternity,
putting each part of my body back together,
and now
these hands hold that of another.
And those hands showed me
how splendid it can be
when you let the right lion search for your honey.

GROWING UP

Bumblebee

Georgia Charlwood

June was alone on the grass in the middle of her garden. One of her chubby hands was buried deep in a jar of squelchy strawberry jam that her mother had left as she ran inside. June was quite content there — testing her finger muscles as she closed and unclosed her fist, feeling the resistance in the jam, and vaguely listening to the shouts from elsewhere in the house.

A flagging bumblebee wriggled towards June through the jungle of grass, captured by the sharp, syrupy scent that also came from a smear down the child's right cheek. The bee was slow and fuzzy and unaware of the curious and clumsy June-giant that had just clocked its presence. A door slammed inside, followed by the smashing of glass and the biggest shout so far. The bee paused on the tip of a dandelion that had sprouted amongst the clean blades. After a moment of contemplation, it elegantly and precisely wiped its antennae through the notches on its front legs.

June watched it for a while longer; its legs picked their way over and under the towering vegetation and its wings twitched and reflected like rainbow glass in the sun. To her, its little body looked soft and squeezable. She retrieved her right hand from the jam just as a car squealed outside, pulling away fast from the house. Finding that the bee was just out of her reach, June excitedly slammed her hands down on the grass, picked up her legs from underneath her and began to crawl towards it. The bee began to scurry the other way. June stretched out a sticky palm towards the fleeing insect and was just about to capture it when a pair of arms swooped down, scooping her up from the grass and into the air.

Grace was gasping. She held her daughter out in front of her; a bruise bloomed purple by her right ear and spilled onto her cheek. Grace's eyes were wild and searching for something — some pain or fear — in that small pink face. A moment passed before she folded into the grass and set June down again at a distance from the now stationary bumblebee.

Licking her finger, Grace lightly rubbed away the drying jam on June's face. Despite knowing that June would not understand her, Grace had many things that she wished she could tell her baby daughter. She found herself failing to find any that would make sense.

Grace spread her pale palms out for her daughter to inspect. June tapped a finger against them playfully, then looked up into her mother's face for the next game. Her mother eclipsed the afternoon sun, her tied back hair outlined with a golden haze as though the whole light from the sky was coming out of her.

"You may not know it yet, but we have the power to do so much with these hands — we can break things and put them back together, we can show our love and we can make others feel pain, we can even end lives with them," said Grace. She put her finger under her daughter's chin and ducked her head so she could meet her eyes more clearly.

When June had been born, she'd been wrapped in a knitted lilac blanket big enough to go twice around her. Placed on her mother's chest, small cheek against collarbones, Grace felt their heartbeats align in faint determination. Ever since that day, it had been just the two of them against the world. Grace often thought that she hadn't really felt anything until her daughter came along.

Grace offered the length of her first finger to the bumblebee. After hesitating for a moment, it crawled onto her smooth skin, twitching its wings. Grace drew her hand carefully up so that the bee was at June's eye-level.

"Whoever made people gave us the power to take others out of existence with our own two hands," said Grace. "We're lucky we've got our own heartbeats and feelings and brains."

June stared intently at the bee but did not try to reach out and touch it. Behind the bee she could still see the silhouette of her mother's face.

"I don't think we should get to decide when others' lives are over, do you?" Grace asked her daughter with a small smile. Her left earring was missing; a smear of blood had escaped from the small hole where a pearl should have been.

A small wind wound its fingers through Grace's hair and kissed the backs of June's knees below her dress. The bumblebee was placed on a cosmos flower at the bottom of the garden. They watched it squirm its way into the centre, before emerging again and, after a pause, taking flight into the next garden.

The jam jar was retrieved from the grass and June was carried into the house. Her mother tiptoed over the shattered glass of the living room door that had spilt into the hallway. Toast was popped up and butter was spread under a thick layer of jam. The pair sat on the kitchen table looking out into the garden, their food in front of them, June's bite-sized squares arranged on the plate in the shape of a flower.

*

June is at her own table now. A glass of wine sits beside her; her briefcase has been thrown onto the chair at the far end of the room. The jungle of plant pots on her patio watch her in the sunlight and she sits, protected by the glass of the windows, watching them back. Then, through dazzling gold, flies a small, dark dot. It lands on the leaf of a violet, resting there for a moment in the warmth, before flying away again. June imagines its wing tracks in the air — the only trace that it leaves — and her mother running out into the street to stop a car from slipping away.

"Take me with you," June whispers to the blue sheet of sky. She gets up and puts some bread in the toaster. The world is a little too big without her mother in it.

The Shoes You Have Lived In

Ellie Eva

Bruised black brogues, the only uniform needed
for racing friends to our favourite swing,
or tumbling, tripping
into a week of bleeding knees
and the stench of antiseptic in a ceramic sink.

Squashy puddle-stained trainers,
springy soles that lift your feet (at eight years old)
on the rain-soaked field
pushing down again and again
until your toes hurt and your lungs burn
crossing that line not quite first but close behind.

A pair of sparkly silver fancy dress heels,
tiny rise kissing the bow of your foot,
telling you *you are grown up now*
as you tap your soles on the neatly tiled floor,
A single pink toenail peeping out, one ankle strap untied.

Beloved, worn and dirty soled,
now the trainers are the ones to carry you.
Don't look too closely, they whisper.
You can almost see the tideline stains
and the unlovely scars
that mar the leather:

reminders, not just of what you have fallen into,

(running down night-cloaked streets, linking arms at
2:33)
but what you have waded through
(the swollen eyes and the *I've had enough now* sighs*).*

Now you really are old enough to choose heels
but instead you keep the greying laces,
cling to the scuffed suede,
carry on walking
and try not to fall.

Last Night

Sebastian Lewis

We shamble-chased
down thin streets, baring
skin in those curt hours
when the night is coldest.

New sounds adorn
old towns shaped from
worn, cream sandstone:
young hearts on parade.

We sang 'til our voices
snapped. We laughed 'til
our chests became concave
with the weight of wheezing.

I ask her for a lighter;
some small sign of community
fostered & kindled
in smoke-curdled words.

I don't smoke. But
the ritual brings me delight. Our cheap cigars
just play at bourgeois decadence:
we make our own stars bloom between our lips.

Magnolia

Emily Black

2015

"I felt as though I were dead," Ruby said, tugging at a knot in her hair. It was short and choppy yet still accumulated tangles. She was not looking at me, or anything for that matter; merely gazing at nothing.

"What did it taste like?"

"Petrol." She spat through her braces, a garish neon pink wire ran across her teeth.

"Well next time your brother buys you some please save me a bit. I want to try vodka." I concluded.

"Elijah gets weird about buying it. He doesn't do it very often. And anyway, you wouldn't like it."

"That's not the point," I said as I ran glittery lipgloss across my chapped lower lip.

We grew up in the towns across from one another, but went to the same school. A half an hour ride in the car if we could nab a lift, or an hour on the bus. I knew Ruby better than I knew my own mother, but when we stopped going to school together we stopped living the same lives. Now aged fourteen, our intermittent catch-ups occurred perhaps twice a year at best. Always in the same park, sat upon a hill arching over the town like the spine of a cat. We sat poised on a bench below a magnolia tree.

"That colour doesn't suit you," Ruby sighed, after a

long pause. She stared at my nail varnish.

I had liked to believe that because of these blunt foundations, we had formed in our formative time together, that when we grew older we would always be able to return to this lovingly plain method. I didn't sugar coat anything for Ruby, and she did the same for me.

When our nail polish debate had died I turned to confide in her: an abrupt turnaround. 'Ruby.'

"Yes?"

"You know Isaac?" Isaac was my boyfriend.

"Yes."

"I don't think I can stand him any more."

She began to howl with laughter.

"No Ruby it's not funny," I protested, "I can't break up with him because I'll have to see him in maths and geography every day."

She laughed even harder.

"This is the hardest thing I have ever had to do!" I snapped.

"Break up with him for Christ's sake." She jumped straight to the endgame. I pouted into the distance, because I knew she was right.

Conversation spiralled around everything from which jeans made us look chubby, to our newly discovered intrigue surrounding hair scrunchies. When she departed, she did so with a vigorous bounce, and disappeared out of sight like a spring. I walked down the other side of the hill and gave the magnolia tree a brief glance before I caught sight of my ride.

2017

Ruby had her braces removed in March. It was May

now, and we had returned to the park for one of our ritual catch ups. It was full of blooming magnolia, verdant pinks flushed through the branches.

We talked about what we want to do after sixth form, life beyond school and the safety of our suburban upbringings. She told me about how she couldn't wait to get out of the town and stop running into the same faces on every street corner. She wanted good grades so she could leave and do something else. Ruby insisted she wouldn't be a store assistant like her mum. She said she was sick of the repetition, sick of the itch which came with living upon this small corner of a map, working at the corner shop on Saturdays.

I told her I had fallen in love. I told her all about Oscar, and how he made me feel. I overflowed with detail and exuberance about this person who had now become the centre of my gravity. I told her about his boyish smile and how he kissed me on the forehead. She smiled and said she was happy for me, but I could tell her mind was elsewhere.

Elijah died last autumn, and Ruby wore the remnants of grief upon her cheeks; her fine greyish skin resembled tissue paper. I was sick to my core thinking about losing a sibling. She told me he went on a night out at one of our few small town clubs and never returned home.

"It's like someone just pressed backspace on his life. A small blip and he was wiped away. It was so fast and so permanent, it was as though he never existed. There was no struggle." She rolled a cigarette: a skill which she told me she learnt how to do from one of her older friends who now left sixth form for university. She pinched the tobacco between her fingers and laid it gently in the paper.

I thought about how Ruby's life got blind-sighted by this domestic tragedy. I almost wished there was some grandeur to her brother's death, for her sake. I sniffed violently whilst gazing at the horizon, in such a way that she couldn't see my eyes well with tears. If there was one thing Ruby and I would never do in front of one another, it was cry.

We sat under the misty veil of her cigarette smoke for a few moments before I announced I had to go and get a lift. We hugged goodbye and she gave me a tissue 'for my cold'. She left with a lethargy, and turning back I could see her wind down the other end of the hill like a tiny pink ant.

2019

Our soft suburban adolescent has reached a crescendo. Now both eighteen we are the peak of our youths, and I know it. It is a delirious summer day in the holidays after our school life has come to an end weeks before. I sip white wine from my plastic cup. Ruby and I split a bottle. My forehead is damp with sweat and we sit aimlessly on that bench once again, like two compass pins pointing at nothing.

All of the hair straightener burns, ruined trainers and tears are streamlined into this moment in which we have returned to the bench on the hill. I bathe in an amber glow from the sun, the same light which gives Ruby's newly bleached hair a honeyed hue. Her hair is still short and choppy but she has grown taller and slimmer over the previous years.

She tells me she fears what is to come. She says some days she wakes up and is unsure whether she can face people, and face trying. She says she is scared to experience, or not experience. Fearful of doing something wrong but equally of missing out.

I point across towards the bottom of the hill, and tell of every finite sign of life on the roads below, all the tiny twitches in the town and the crossing paths of each person. But equally, I tell her I understand.

"Oscar broke up with me," I say.

"Oh god are you serious?"

I nod, recalling the way my heart plummeted to the centre of the earth when the love I had become so accustomed to was snatched from my veins.

"He didn't deserve you anyway." Ruby wraps me in an all encompassing hug, winding her arms around my back. I laugh, a choked laugh, but a laugh nonetheless.

"You should have told me sooner," she says. She crunches the plastic from her cup of wine in her fist.

"Does it get easier? This loss," I ask.

"Yes."

"I know it's not the same, but do you still miss Elijah?"

"Yes."

I can feel the weight of our endeavours bearing down upon my body like pressure underwater. Every lighthearted friendship turned bitter, every sour swig from a bottle under red lights at parties, each moment spent applying pearlescent eyeshadow in the hopes of catching the right attention. Every day off school for lack of wanting to leave the solace of a bed, every indignant tear shed in silence, every time we told her parents we were at a friend's house when we were elsewhere. Over the years, we become an amalgamation of each broken fingernail, each I love you spoken aloud and every melancholy lesson learnt.

Ruby glares out over the horizon, as though she is about to fight it. Throwing fists at the border between the rooftops and the clouds. A caramel twilight ascends upon the restless heat. The sky is a milky pink, and our breathing is slow but succinct. I watch a bus pull out on a street below the hill, and I wonder where it is going.

Final Year

James Wijesinghe

They used to ask me what I want to be when I'm older,
But now they ask about next year.
This morning I could hear
The Future whisper on the horizon, "Go to London."
By the evening it cried in my ear, "Get to work."

If I don't pursue what it wants, do my passes have a
purpose?
Were these classes then all worthless?
No, they mark sections of a journey.
Cos with time there's no end, it's just something that
starts,
So what you become when you're older, will be whenever
you are.

HEALTH

ROYAL UNITED HOSPITAL, 1997

Bethany Saunders

When Hale-Bopp crossed the sky,
Dad's fleece jacket frayed at the edges:
his mind dilated into numbness.
When Hale-Bopp hit earth's axis,
its siren culled the blood-moon
from its fraught position above us.
The telescope lens closed over.
Mum keeled under. When the comet
crossed our eye-line, my cries
measured 60 kilometres in diameter.
Mum took Dad's hand, she worried
it tighter. When Hale-Bopp
reached our orbit I was a bud / brand new,
half-the-radius of the umbilical
bruise left at the base of Mum's stomach.
When Hale-Bopp crossed the sky
my parents wound the vowels I emptied
into a single, trailing sound.
A sound they prayed would carry.

Milk

Milan George

He is afraid that her white stomach
will ripen,
stilling blood-black waters
and staining sheets.

He can just about see faint periwinkle lines,
stretched
over hips.

Later, two hot drinks are placed on a table.
They both stir.
They see a navel form, a deep mound
inverted in milk.
Never-mind,
the skin has gone now—
scraped away the layers with a silver spoon.

The Unbecoming Beret

Lillie Elsworth

There is no suitable way
to wear a red beret
to a sexual health clinic.

Like a scarecrow at a crucifixion,
it makes a mockery of the blood
and crowning.

You go with the nurse in rubber shoes.
I wait with other men
and HPV posters.

I wince at the white smell,
fill in the paperwork
and tick for deliverance.

Please Wait By the Line

Jessica White

I know all of the comings and goings of this station. I see it every day. In the early hours, the business men and women hurry down the platform in that half-walk half-run they do, briefcases in hand, and their eyes widen as they watch the train doors shut off their passage. I can't help but chuckle when someone just misses it. *Better luck next time, mate.* Isn't life just cruel like that sometimes? If they'd have just got there a few seconds earlier, they would have leapt over the gap and through those doors just in time. It's like watching some tragic Shakespeare play. What if Juliet had woken up a few seconds earlier? Would she still have found Romeo dead? *What if? What if? What if?* The world is full of people wondering just that, but there is no real point in dwelling on it. Life goes on.

The clock ticks by to the lunchtime roar and the crowd thickens with the tourists; they all stare at the upside down maps in their hands, perplexed by the complex zigging and zagging that confronts them. Often, they ask me how to get to the place where they want to go and I try my best to direct them, but, in all honesty, I don't see much of the city outside of this station. This is all I know. The familiar hustle and bustle of the comings and goings is all I need to know. And, of course, there are the large school groups with small children weaving in and out of the hustle and bustle, and the teacher's eyes widen as they watch one child stray too near to the edge.

Mind The Gap. I shout on repeat like a broken record. *Please Wait By The Line.*

I point to the smudged yellow line that is in dire need of renewing. This whole place is in need of that as it wilts and rots due to the stomping and stamping of all the daily hustle and bustle. I probably need it too. But this is all I know.

Life goes on. Life goes on. Life goes on. The day passes and the hustle and bustle dies down to a mere whisper. Only a few stray travellers hover on the platform in the cool, dark hours of the night. Here, they wait, in a station of the lonesome, wrapped up in their thick wool coats to keep out the cold that would brush the wounds on their skin with its cruel hands if they let it. Their hats pulled down so low they blind them, hands shoved under armpits, scarves slowly choking the life out of them, and feet stepping from side to side to avoid being frozen for eternity. Waiting. Forever waiting. "For what?" I hear you ask. Nothing. Absolutely nothing. Everyone on this platform is waiting for the same thing. But if that same thing is no thing, then it would be a reasonable question to ask why they are waiting at all? They are all waiting, perhaps unconsciously, for something incredible to happen. Like the blackest black of the universe before the beginning of time, hovering, existing, reducing, sitting still and zooming all at once, waiting for that spark. The spark that became something so beautiful, and yet, so revolting at the same time. That's what they are waiting for. They all seem to be waiting for their lives to begin even when they have already begun.

As I scan the faded yellow line that they all stand behind, I hover my gaze over a woman who looks so strangely ordinary. I say strangely because it is her ordinariness that makes her stand out. She hunches over with her hands clasped together in front of her and pulls at the old skin hanging off her thumb, seeming completely mesmerised by it. A flexibility of the skin separate from the bone that comes with age. Suddenly, her head jerks up and she looks directly at me. Now, I can see the grey skin underneath her eye drooping like an old plastic bag, giving away the things that she shouldn't have done which now cause the body to visibly wilt and rot. The dull glint in her eye shows a lost hope for the spark, and yet, she still waits. She must have felt me staring at her. Isn't it strange how they all seem to have a sense of being watched even when there is nobody around? There are eyes watching in the white walls, ears listening for an echo in the halls, a mouth sitting at the edge of the window pane that calls. No one is ever truly alone.

Further along, there is a chap who looks fresh out of the factory, all spick and span. He stands tall and mighty with hair perfectly gelled back, cheekbones that look as though they have been sculpted by a sculptor, and glowing teeth that are so blindingly white that you can barely see the pain that lies behind them. You're probably wondering how I know there is pain. To that, I chuckle, because there is always pain of one sort or another. Everyone has their secrets. I see it day in and day out. All the travellers pass me by with that same photocopied smile plastered on their faces. It's the same smile that you can find everywhere from the cover of magazines to the perfectly coded images that scroll across your screen for hours every day. But images don't cry after the face is made. So, this is it. This is what we've made.

Please Wait By The Line!

"God, when is this bloody train gonna get here?!" The sudden shriek comes from a funny looking girl with bright red hair and neon leg warmers. She stomps and stamps around the platform like an elephant at a tea party with the neon jumping up and down and up and down. As I watch her pink trainers stray over the line, I open my mouth to shout. But the other girl who was stood with her drags her back before any sound escapes my lips. I inwardly breathe a sigh of relief. For now, I am satisfied.

I continue to stare at the two girls for a while longer with my focus particularly on the other girl instead of the one who was making a fuss. Apart from appearing to be getting increasingly annoyed with her friend, the girl had a reserved look about her. Her dark eyebrows were furrowed, hiding her steel-coated eyes that might have been rather pretty if the rest of the world were allowed to see them. Why doesn't she smile? Girls always look their prettiest when they are smiling. A smile is the best make-up a girl could wear! She's in the prime of her life! This is the only time that she will be most attractive to the opposite sex!

"Give us a smile, love," I say in the hope of installing some kind of joy in her. But I am met with silence and a withering look that would have made me wilt and rot even further if it could. It seems she has been plagued by that common affliction nowadays which they call 'resting bitch face'. It's a shame, really. All these young girls scowling at all of the comers and goers. Laughter is a foreign language to them. Their lips are sealed in a permanent flatline. Were they always like this? No, they can't have been. They were born screaming and alive, but look at them now. They've learned to warn them off. It's protection.

Please Wait By The Line!

The line, the line, the line, the line, the line. Some poor sod will have painted the yellow years ago because somebody tall and mighty like that spick and span chap told him to. And now, everyone must stand by it. Those are the rules. No ifs. No buts. And if someone were to ever dare stray out of line, the result would be catastrophic. For what is the world without the line? Without the line, it would just be a blank platform for all of the hustle and bustle to stomp and stamp wherever they please with no consideration for both their own and other's safety. It would be chaos, I tell you! No, the line must be there. I am thankful for the line. It brings me comfort. Knowing where I stand. Knowing where they all must stand. Side by side by side by side by side.

Tonight is the night. I am certain of it. I can tell it is going to happen because the station sings a special song. The sound of fluid dripping onto the floor, *drip drip drip*, chimes with those feet rhythmically stepping from side to side, *step step step*, as the rusted metal track creaks that familiar creak, *creak creak creak*. One of them is going to do it. End it all. But which one? Will it be the old woman with the drooping grey skin and the dull eyes filled with lost hope? Or will it be the spick and span chap with the screwed on smile? Or, perhaps, the girl with the bitch face as she grows impatient with her friend who doesn't seem to be much of a friend at all? Or maybe she'll shove her in. Now, that'd be a laugh. But wait, what about that train conductor with the reflective vest? He spends his days watching the coming and going ons of this wilting and rotting station as he himself wilts and rots with it, never having anything better to do than to shout at the hustle and bustle.

Please Wait By The Line. Please Wait By The Line. Please Wait By The Line.

PURPOSE, DECISIONS

Thought Contagion

David Marallag

invasive thoughts
have invaded my mind
evade these flailing thoughts
with a brain as frail as mine
failing but i'm rather fine
to finally understand
this flayed and finite life
thinking since every last night
think if this is my last night
as i turn off that night light
if i would wake up in fright
only to see that last light
that door, beaming light
that tunnel, that some kind of spiritual funnel
actually I don't
understand it as much
i'm always under
standing beneath
the knowledge of such
hanging on this ledge
letting go
at life's slightest touch
no answer
no solution
i'd rather find
those minute resolutions
and keep that pace

i guess i do know
to some extent
thinking that i don't
hoping that i won't
because ignorance is bliss
a mouthful you'll never miss
from mouths, in platitudes remiss
and unquoted, go amiss
for they rationalise the absurd
this life that can't be put into words
no I don't know anything at all
i'd leave it at that and that's my call
and leave it to life's whims
for nothing is ever as it seems

Schachspielers

Rachael Brown

In the square outside Freiheit street number sixteen,
in the world above U-Bahn commuters, there meet
the Schachspielers.

Some say, in fact, they never leave,
but boiled kneecaps and brittle bones
once buried in the cheap concrete
now rise daily to enthrone two kings.

Gnarled they are in build and limp,
each man's spine a humped back bridge
in dated shirts that no longer fit but ripple
in the rumble of the underground
beneath.

Shuffling over the arrival of the 6:33,
Tuesday's chosen enthroned ones, assemble armies:
a wooden bishop with a chip on his shoulder,
a pawn with a bash on the head waits for orders
as spectators sit.

Now player one was once a handsome man—
six feet in height with a healthy tan,
but his skin the wind, and rain's pulled down
like candle wax. On his finger sags
a cigarette butt.

On the opposite side of the chequered battleground,
playing black, player two's a used tissue kinda man
with a scrunched-up face and ferocious brows
that quiver as he thinks.

The game begins
with the movement of his feet — two leather slippers
thoughtfully complete the ruler length
to his kingside pawn three.

In the time it takes to bend his knees
and tune his vertebrae in squeaks,
the U6 bursts its banks
and spills commuters up the ramps,
their fingers flashing, tapping, Google Map-bashing,
speed walking, text-talking, Whats-app-apping
or they're Snapchatting, networking, Insta-picture-filter-
picking,
ghosting or they're roasting someone, swiping left or
right in tandem,
facelessly Face Timing, Facebooking, Face-swapping,
fucking Amazon-ing
and it's all gone
in the time it takes player two to straighten up.
Not hook-up, book a check-up, skype a break-up, apply
make-up
just straighten up.

The streets hush.
Player one's back cracks as he breaks ranks
to let the queen through, coughs twice,
adjusts his tie and recedes
in a puff of smoke.

In the Heart of Ho Chi Min

Ben Bampton

Rammed to the hilt with peddlers, vendors, backpackers, bikes, vans, buses, Saigon's Pham Ngu Lao is a hub of local and foreign activity. The offices of bus companies open their doors onto this busy street, spilling cartloads of passengers out and onto the latest departure with clockwork consistency. The street brims with activity even in the lapses between buses. Carts and vans shunt their backs onto the pavements, hurriedly loaded with some delivery or other. The locals doing the loading are young, but no less adept at smoking their cigarettes while working than the older men — the drivers — who chuff from their front seats. The smell of their cigarettes, made more pungent by the humidity, floats into the air and carries down the road, jostling with the smell of cooking noodles and petrol fumes for attention. The suppliers of these other smells dot themselves along the pavement: local wives offer over-ripe fruit and dishes on demand from their mobile stations and shopfronts; motorcyclists pull up, navigating the hectic pavement surface to find a space to park. Through all this, the backpackers join the mill — one eye on the roadside, the other on the shopfronts — in their attempt to find travel to the next place. Few are intense as Saigon.

The Submarine

Harriet Cornwell

Silence. Peace. Panic.
Our steel shell sinks into the abyss
As we glide unseen through yielding waters.
Three inches from death with our world-ending weapons
Hidden away, an apocalypse at our fingertips, waiting for
the call.

The stale air makes claustrophobia a worse enemy.
Madness tapping at the windows.
The darkness drips in, drip… drip… drowning
the twitching lights. In my head,
Sanity corrodes like iron in saltwater.

Through the creaking glass is black and blue.
All that I can see: sea. Sea. The bottom of the deep
blue…
I am not a sailor, whose white suit mimics his billowing,
birdlike sails.
I am a prisoner. My steel chains mimic my cell.
This submarine is not yellow, but grey.

Submerged in a sense of stasis.
We have not sunk to the lowest point, nor have we
floated to the surface,
But we stay, average, dull, in the middle, never rising,
never falling,
Drifting in a passive state.

Waiting.

Pulled Over

E.C. Ryder

Red and blue streaks fluttered across the rain-soaked rear window. The wipers to my '78 Buick waved furiously as they sent great swaths of water either side of my car. The sirens had died now, replaced by the pitter-patter of rain, the squeak of wipers, and my own rapid breathing. I felt the slam of a car door and without looking, knew the cop was walking to my window. It was at this point I began running through the different paths this encounter might take.

The cop, face blank, knocked on the driver side window with his flashlight. His eyes swivelled in his skull, searching the visible contents of the Buick. But he saw nothing. I rolled down the window, and said: "Hello, officer. Is there a problem?" The problem was my speed. Fifteen over. He gave me a ticket, 300 bucks, and then I was on my way. The four kilos of coke poorly covered by a jacket in the back seat went undiscovered. So too did the bullet-riddled body of a drug dealer in the trunk.

The cop, face blank, knocked on the driver side window with his flashlight. Immediately, he caught sight of the coke, whipped out his pistol, and pointed it at me. "Sir I'm gonna need you to get out of the car right now!" I got out and he shoved me against the wet, rusted metal of my Buick as he clipped a pair of handcuffs around my wrists and told me my rights.

The cop, face blank, knocked on the driver side window with his flashlight. His eyes widened as he glimpsed the white bricks in the back seat and before he could do or say anything, I pulled the trigger to the .44 Magnum that had been pressed discretely against the car door. Metal and plastic ripped outward as the bullet shot through the door and smacked into the cop's kneecap. Bone and muscle and ligament were obliterated and the cop buckled to the black pavement with an agonised grunt. I kicked the door open and shot him through the eye, watching with grim satisfaction as blood bubbled and streaked into the water.

The cop, face blank, knocked on the driver side window with his flashlight...

Infinitesimal

Isabella Drage

I wish I could live through something.
I'm trying to fold truth from fiction like how we used to crook our fingers into
church spires, over and over, reaching inside for something hidden. you know
how it was, that tireless game.
I remember when writing was burrowing for precious metals, searching
for something that winked when it caught the light, kaleidoscopic colours
in the fish-eyed lens of childhood, every action more consequential.
I wrote in oil, set my words on fire and told myself
the whole world would read by my flame: quick lick of a spark,
burst of hot air, never look back — *exhale.*
I'm still grappling for words, still pretending to have a greater understanding of the universe
than everyone else, when really all I know is that today is a Wednesday,
and life is just a one-take movie of todays and tomorrows that bleed
into each other, too nauseating to look at except
from the corner of your eye.

sometimes, I still ache to be seen.
other days I want nothing more than to push the little

boat of my body
gently out to sea, watch it fade into a pinprick from the
shore. we are all
so small, and vigorously striving not to be, but isn't it a
relief?
these clumsy fingerprints are quickly covered by moss
and scrubby earth,
winter will strip our memory to a carcass, and then—
nothing.

but I'm grateful for this small parcel of time. forget
gemstones;
I'm trying to press the flowers that sneak between the
pavestones.
let's pause a while, cup an afternoon in our hands and
watch it slip
through our fingers, nurturing what it is to feel
powerless.
today, I tried to picture all the particles of dust flocking
to form our bodies like starlings in murmurations.
I feel so very small, and these words won't mold to my
will,
red-white-hot on the page. sincerity is hard to come by,
even
in conversations with myself.
but here I am,
and there you are,
and isn't that something worth shouting about?

please, stay a while.

RELIGION

Mother Moon

Lily Proctor

On the first day, God screwed the lightbulb in
and flicked the switch. Afterwards, he made you,
then kicked his feet up on the couch
to let you finish it all off.
On the second day, you made everything
grey turn green. For a while, God had assumed himself
colour-blind, and watched with envy as the world
sprouted beneath you; the light
given something to look at.
The third and fourth were much the same,
you named the ocean and the great plains
and became the reason for stars,
and they then learnt what it means to be worded.

You made people, on the fifth day.
You made them laugh and cry and ache
and do what living people do,
which is to be selfish sometimes:
to like sex and chocolate and rollercoasters and beer,
and you were so good at this.
And you loved them so much.
So, on the sixth day you gave birth to your love
and she loved you back. And you tried again,
and he died. And you tried a third time,
and she was born too, fashioned from your quiet grief
in a shape that made it bearable.

And on the seventh day, you barely
took a break. Though your work was done,
though we were being cruel and remarkable
in the language you invented for us,
you still knocked at God's shins
with the vacuum cleaner

as you swept up the left-over dust.

What Lies in God's Wake

Aayushi Jain

1

Bedtime is my favourite part of the day. That's when Mum comes to kiss me goodnight, always exactly in the middle of my forehead. She bends down. Her hair falls around my face, enclosing me like the leaves of a willow tree. Soft light filters through the strands. I close my eyes and let her leaves brush my cheek.

One morning, before school, I ask why she kisses me there. "It's your third eye," she says, braiding my hair. "When I kiss it, it opens." I think about this throughout the day. At night, after she leaves my room, I reach up from under the covers and carefully touch my forehead, feeling for eyelashes.

I wish my third eye could help me fall asleep. My parents close their bedroom door and lower their voices, but Mum always gets louder and louder until she is shouting. She is wind slapping against the side of my face. Dad never shouts, but he is the deep rumble of an earthquake that makes me grip the bedsheets. Then, it stops. Sometimes that's even worse — the silence afterwards. I try not to imagine what their faces look like when they're angry, and I count the teddy bears on the wallpaper until I fall asleep.

2

I'm sleeping. I know I'm sleeping but I can't wake up. I am a spider trying to climb my cobweb up to the moon, but the sea won't let me. It keeps throwing up frozen daggers of water that cut my legs off, one by one. But every time I lose a leg, it grows back again, so I keep climbing. I climb for hours, while the moon smiles down at me and the sea glares up and my legs fall again and again into the dark water like matchsticks.

When the dream finally ends, I roll out of bed and creep across the landing to my parents' room. They are sleeping with their backs to each other, with so much space between them that there would be enough room for thousands of me. I crawl into the valley between their bodies, and they roll over towards me. They are half-asleep and each of them clumsily swings an arm across my stomach, one after the other. I stare in disbelief at their giant hands in front of me, clasping each other as if it were completely natural. This is the closest I have seen them.

3

It's Saturday and I am wearing billowing harem pants that smell like India, like red clay and saffron, like fresh lotuses in monsoon season. Dad is out running errands, and Mum sits in the chaise, reading Kamala Markandaya's *Nectar in a Sieve*. I run around the house pretending to be a genie, granting wishes to potted ficuses and grandmother's blue china. I run past Mum and ask what her wish is, and she catches me by my waist, pulling me close.

"You," she whispers. I sink into her arms. She smells like sandalwood. I am a tiny, happy genie. She is the warm lamp I curl into at night.

4

"Go ask Dad if he's having dinner." I feel my shoulders shoot up. This is my least favourite part of the day. Sometimes when Mum cooks dinner, Dad pretends he's not hungry. I walk to the lounge as slowly as I can. Today the TV is on and so is his phone screen, but he isn't looking at either. Instead, his eyes flicker back and forth between thoughts, and the knots above his eyebrows bulge, deepening the lines across his forehead. I stare at them. His forehead is a wrinkled carpet I can never pull straight.

As I get closer, the smell of smoke and breath-mints fills my nostrils. I know the answer is 'No'. But I ask him anyway, and when he says he's not hungry, I still feel my stomach drop. For the rest of the evening, Mum is angry. I know this because she asks me questions I don't know the answer to, like "Why do I bother?" When we sit down to eat, I eat twice as much food as I usually do, hoping it will make up for Dad, but she doesn't notice.

Later, as she is kissing me goodnight, we hear him rustling in the kitchen cupboard for food. I watch her lips tighten at the sound. Tonight, when they fight, they forget to close the door. I cover my ears but I can still hear them.

Wind stings my cheek. "I'm leaving!" it screams. My third eye trembles and pulses like a warning sign.

5

On Sunday Mum takes me swimming. She swims in the adult lanes and I play at the shallow end, by the steps, swinging between the railings and pretending to be a monkey. My arm-bands are yellow and see-through, and when I look through them everything changes shape. The lifeguard turns into a lifeguard-shaped balloon. Suddenly I feel sad and I don't know why, so I swim over to Mum's lane. I hold my breath, slip under the surface, and watch her underwater. She swims toward and away. She glows like a jellyfish. The water cradles me in its blue, swinging belly.

6

Today in History, we learn about the Greek Gods. Poseidon is my favourite. We make posters, and Miss Arnold stands behind me and asks why I've drawn everyone with three eyes. Her face is scrunched up like a dried leaf. When I explain, she holds up my poster to the class and says, "Make your pictures realistic." Everyone laughs. She's smiling and looking over their heads. I wonder if anyone has ever kissed her on her forehead. On the bus ride home, I draw everyone's third eye back in.

Mum doesn't answer the doorbell. I reach into the plant pot and pull out the spare key. I find her in the spare bedroom, lying awake with the covers drawn up to her cheeks. I ask if she knows about Poseidon. She doesn't say anything, so I shake her gently. She smiles, but her eyes stay frozen. They are still and glazed like empty snow globes. I know she has been crying and I try to kiss her forehead, but she turns away. I wish I was Poseidon.

Then, I could control all the water in the world, and she would never cry.

7

Mum is still upstairs. She is on the phone to Grandma. When she doesn't come down, Dad and I have microwave macaroni for dinner.

"Why is Mum talking to Grandma?" "She isn't feeling well." "Will she still come kiss me goodnight?" "Yes." "Why isn't she feeling well?" "She just needs someone to talk to." "Can't she talk to you?"

His eyes drop to the floor, and he turns away. He is looking out the kitchen window at something, but it's pitch black outside.

8

I lie in bed, listening for her footsteps. When she comes, I quickly pretend to be asleep. She brushes hair from my face. Her lips feel cool against my forehead, like moonlight. I keep my eyes closed, but as she is walking away they snap open, searching for her in the dark. My lips move without me wanting them to: "This is my favourite part of the day." She stands in the doorway, looking back, an expression on her face I haven't seen before.

I dream of God. I am sitting in a boat in the middle of an ocean at night, staring up. I try to move my neck but it is stuck. My third eye is wide open and I can't blink. The moon is bright and it swings above me from left to right, to left, to right... God is a hypnotist dangling his watch from the sky.

9

Dad opens the door when I come home from school. When I look in his eyes he gives me a strange smile. I follow him to the kitchen and watch him take macaroni out of the freezer.

"Where's Mum?" "At Grandma and Grandpa's." His eyes flicker back and forth but the smile stays stuck to his face.

"Can we go?" He shakes his head. He is smiling the same way he smiles at strangers. "Is she bringing back dessert? "She's going to stay there." His eyes dart between my face and the window. "... Like a sleepover?" He stares at the floor. "For how long?" He is standing at the kitchen counter, his hands gripping the edge. His smile shakes. It collapses and rebuilds itself over and over again.

"When is she coming back?" He swallows. "I don't know." His face twitches. His voice sounds like something is stuck in his throat, and I realise it is sadness. I press myself into his body and his arms wrap around me. He doesn't cry but I feel his chest heaving like an ocean.

10

That night, I climb into bed with Dad and lie still. He closes his eyes and pretends to sleep. As I start to fall asleep, I think I hear her footsteps on the stairs, and I bolt upright.

"Just the dishwasher," he says sadly.

I lie back down. I draw my hand from under the

covers and bring a fingertip to my lips. I kiss it silently and touch it to the middle of my forehead. I can feel my third eye, wet and blinking in the dark like a lighthouse. God is a storm, and I am a lighthouse. She is the spinning ship I search for at night.

Fantasia

Ed Alexander

I stared listlessly at the darkness beyond my window, the faint reflection of my face in the glass, and nothing else. The canvas was almost entirely black, the monotony broken only by the occasional glimpse of my more prominent features; the bridge of my nose, the jut of my jaw, the furrows of my brow in the limelight.

Only the left side of my face was visible, bathed in light by the delicate flicker of a lightbulb. Once or twice I caught sight of a glimmer in my left eye, cornflower blue lost in shade. I had become *The Phantom*, my opera now a chorus of internal chatter.

After mere seconds or an entire lifetime, I grew tired of reflecting upon my reflection.

What good could come of this overthinking?

I lurched from my seat and moved to kill the light, but the bulb beat me to it. The glass shattered with a quiet *bang* and left me floating in shadow.

How wonderful, a private supernova for my eyes only.

I felt privileged to witness such a performance… for all of one second. I took a deep breath, then decided to answer the call of my mattress. As I undressed I felt increasing judgement, bordering on a slight anxiety. There was no one else in the building and yet it was as though eyes pierced me from the corners and crevices of the room.

I slid under the comfort, protection and care of the duvet.

Jesus Christ, that hurt! My palm… what the f**k is in my palm?

I remained blind but was certain that this was not my bed and I was not in my room. Relaxation had morphed into anguish that repeated itself three more times — in my other hand and then in each foot. The pain ploughed into me from nowhere. A suffering unlike anything I had ever experienced before. Agony and throbbing flooded through my extremities as each was stretched outwards until I stood in an 'X' position. My limbs felt stunted, weaker, strange — almost childlike.

Where had my calm cradle gone?

The sudden blaze of overhead floodlights soon answered my question. Tears had long-since filled my eyes, yet I could still make out the blurred image of my bed being wheeled through an immense metallic door. A great grey door in a great grey wall in the expanse of a great grey warehouse. It was a museum of fantastic, suffocating dullness.

Tilting my head backwards I could barely make out the roof that soared high into the heavens. Through teary eyes I saw her. That radiant maiden. Her face had an undeniable glow, her smile the delightful centrepiece. The remainder of her appearance was irrelevant — all that mattered was that delicate smile and those kind eyes. When she kissed my cheek and wiped away a droplet I forgot about the stakes in my hands and feet. I forgot about my distress and confusion. She would protect me.

Lost in the allure of this woman I had failed to see the shadows closing in, encircling. It was only when a featureless hand fell upon her shoulder that I sensed the threat. Before I could protest she gave the silhouette a knowing nod and exited the door that had swallowed my bed.

The lights that hung from above intensified, causing me to squint. In a haze, I was twirled around by the faceless figures and met with the sight of a thousand other children who had also been nailed to their own personal saltire. They faced forward, their gazes hidden from mine, but I could hear a chorus of fretful breaths and I saw a sea of squirms. They all wore black — black belts matched with black shorts matched with black shirts matched with black futures… trapped within this great grey warehouse. A truly vibrant image.

All were arranged in equidistant rows and columns, a chessboard where all the pieces were pawns.

Some may have called the symmetry artful, a genius expression of the mind. Some.

They wheeled me into position in a tight gap at the back of the arrangement, my wounds still pulsating.

This is Hell.

As those firm hands slipped off of my wooden cross and left me in place, a different woman stepped onto a dais at the front of the assembly. She was not golden, but rather dressed in a rustic brown overcoat. Where she had been luminous, this new woman was plain. But what warmth she lacked in appearance, she made up for in voice.

As she opened her mouth, hypnotic lullabies filled the air, enchanting my peers like a Siren on jagged rocks. Grace personified. All were amazed. All, that is, barring myself and a freckled girl with fiery hair a few rows and columns away. As the others listened in awe to that sweetest of music, my partner and I raged against the bars that were hammered through our skin, bone, tendons, and muscle. Agony erupted, butt it was worth it a thousand times over. I would sooner die than join these mindless drones.

Predictably, the silhouettes returned to my side and that of the ginger girl, the girl ablaze. That inferno was soon extinguished with horrendous ease, scissors sweeping like scythes to strip off the red river flowing from her scalp. The fight went out of her as I continued to writhe, doing so until I felt a sharp piercing sensation in my neck and then a weakness flooding my consciousness. I was simultaneously struggling and submitting, alert yet drowsy.

I will rage against the dying of the light. I will rage… I will…

An unknown length of time later, I forced my eyes open and prayed that the nightmare was over. I yearned for my blanket. I must have still been dreaming — no waking moment was this grim, grisly, and bleak. Still adjusting to the glaring light, I felt the iron nails that held me in place and the course wood chafing my skin.

Have mercy.

I fully adjusted my vision to the sun's rays that were beating my naked, sullen husk of a body. I found myself on a mound of dirt, scarcely covered by clumps of crocodile-green grass. Around me was a barren wilderness that floated off endlessly.

Two hills broke the uniformity, standing a mile or so in front of me with a cavernous valley between us. Each stood perhaps half-a-mile away.

A bizarre sight lay atop each of these mounds, familiar structures crowning them — on the left, my childhood home and, on the right, the church I had once attended.

In my confusion, I had almost forgotten the burning sensation pulsating from my hands and feet. Two winged demons swept in from behind me, landing one on each hand. A stunning mural of crimson and gold on the right, a haunting ghost of onyx on the left. A Phoenix and a Raven.

Half in desperation and half in dread, I screeched in an incomprehensible tongue, crying for help and hope. The Raven twisted to look directly at me, through me, revealing one twinkling eye and one empty socket. I felt a rush of heat from the other direction, turning to observe the Phoenix, the bird now suddenly ablaze. It was brilliant, ecstatic.

My admiration was soon charred to ash as my skin blistered, drawing more shrieks from my heavy lungs. The piercing sound sent both birds flying in a haze of black and red.

Tortured by the nails, scalded skin, and my own weight, I looked on weakly as the creatures soared towards separate hilltops. Torpedoing, they streamed onwards and onwards until violently smashing into the church and the house. It was cataclysmic, thrusting me backwards into the cross that bore me, briefly lifting the punishing weight from my wounds.

The church, which had been drummed into by the Raven, was now veiled in an impenetrable dust that grew, soon towering high into the heavens. As that smoking monster swelled and rose, its brother awakened. What had once been my home now became a furnace, hissing and howling against the smog. Light and dark intertwined, mating and warring all at once.

Exhaustion took hold of me and I lost my thoughts and feelings in the titanic battle. There was no let up until the sun, a powerless bystander, dropped below the horizon, still trembling.

Night reigned. Silence presided over the wilderness I

found myself in. The stars scintillated in the sky, painting the story of the cosmos in cryptic myths. Behind those dwindling fires there was an inky quilt. The constellations were gleaming beads sewn onto the darkness that gave me an inexplicable drop of hope. A drop that grew. And grew some more. Perhaps it would soon fill me completely and perhaps it would not. Regardless, I left behind all concerns and fear in that moment, focusing on the cosmos.

The dread of further punishment, something I had previously been washed away with, had dissipated. I was present.

No wonder the stars inspired tales across all eras and cultures, from Aboriginal Dreamtime to Ancient Egyptian mythology.

In that darkness, consumed by shadow, my spirit had risen. My breathing, previously so laboured, returned to a calm tranquillity. I felt lighter. I felt an emerging freedom. As the returning sun swept away the stars, I was reminded of the battle that had taken place the day before. In the obscurity and majesty of the night, I had lost both sight and thought of war. Now I remembered as my gaze fell upon a pair of lifeless, decrepit ruins. Debris covered the leftmost mound, whilst its opposite was naught but charred, half-eaten walls and impenetrable black. Two shattered faces, once glorious and comely, wailed at me from across the barren valley.

And I was no longer alone. Warm smiles shone up at me and smooth hands held my weight. Physically and mentally drained, I had believed it to be an illusion, the dark seemingly playing tricks on *all* of my senses. But I was wrong. They had been the hope that had trickled through my soul. They would free me from the horror. Desolation and salvation had hidden side-by-side in the obscurity of that night.

The pain of removing the stakes in my hands and feet was nothing compared to the relief of being released from that cross. I collapsed face-first into the dirt and dug my fingers into the dusty earth. I inhaled deeply, collecting as much dust in my lungs as fresh air, but it mattered little.

I wretched quite disgustingly, unintentionally signalling to my friends that I wanted water. My lungs, coated in filth, felt more open and more pure than I could previously remember. Bringing myself to kneel, head rocking backward, I poured the water carelessly over my face. Some quenched my thirst, some cooled my singed forehead, and some merely cascaded over my naked body. I'm sure my saviours didn't see the tears that were lost in the waterfall plummeting onto me.

The nightmare appeared to be over, but the dream continued. They helped lift me up, though I struggled and stumbled under the weight of fatigue. Casting an eye back to the wastes atop the hills I spied a silhouette upon each.

I turned to the man over whom I had wrapped an arm, his face so comely. He nodded in silence, allowing a faint look of joy to appear in his expression. It was only fleeting, yet I was certain of its existence and meaning. I stepped forward and we began an arduous, taxing journey down the valley and then back up.

I was out on my feet, resting almost all of my weight — both bodily and emotional — upon this nameless Samaritan and his jubilant helpers. When I could carry myself independently my movement was sloth-like. In the bottom of the basin I glanced up at the climb that was still to come and considered resting there, but I found courage in the memory of the ground that I had already covered, ignoring the fact that that had been downhill — it was still progress.

If I stop now, I will never start again.

At the summit of the first hill, upon which had once been a church, I was met with a loving gaze. It held me, warmed me, and released the soreness in my entire body. The gaze belonged to a magnificent statue, carved with intricate detail and delicate precision. The man it depicted was dark-skinned, had flowing black locks, and a grand beard covering his cheeks and chin. Through that bush of hair, I made out a tender smile matched in his walnut eyes. I knew not who he was, yet his message was clear. From his core pervaded an ineffable benevolence that resonated deep inside my own heart. On his outstretched arms perched two diminutive birds — that very same Raven, now paired with a snowy Dove. In opposition, yet at peace. I laughed with love and delight. I knew where I needed to go and whirled towards the other mound.

The hike from one top to the other was marvellous, each of my steps along the way creating a ripple of green growth in the earth around it. As *I* energised the terrain, *it* rejuvenated me.

Just before completing the climb I swivelled to look across the wilderness; it had exploded into a fertile savannah, a veritable nirvana. I had ventured from the bowels of a ferocious, malicious beast to the cradling arms of a gentle mother. A handful of steps followed and I was there, the mountain had been conquered.

There she was once more, that radiant maiden, waiting. Bathed in light, she stood outside my rebuilt house, somehow restored to its former glory. I hugged her tightly, intending to never let go.

Home.

My eyes opened gradually, the bedsheets wrapped snugly over my body. They were temporarily blinded by the light shining through my window. Regaining my sight, I glanced at the shattered bulb on my desk and then at the branches bustling in a breeze outside my window.

Morning.

Hell Fled

Lucie Hynes

The angel Virgil gazed down from where she stood at the top of one of the many trees of Eden, a crease between her eyebrows, evidently displeased with what she saw. She curled her lip at the spectacle of Adam and Eve gambolling about beneath her like fools, Eve brandishing a bunch of grapes and occasionally throwing one into the gaping mouth of Adam, who laughed and leapt about like a maniac. Virgil sighed and soared away from the sight that was so contemptible to her. She soon found herself with two of her angel brethren, Cadriel and Gabriel, who were in the midst of discussing the subjects she had just fled from, and their perceived threat from the fallen angel, Lucifer.

"Have you seen him?" Cadriel was saying. "He crouches in the form of a bird in a tree some miles from here. No doubt our Lord shall be dispirited by his presence. All I can hope is that those wingless fools do not take him at his word. He's bound to try and trick them, and frankly, they're not very intelligent."

"Don't speak so!" cried Virgil, frowning at Cadriel despite the fact that he voiced her inner thoughts. "They were created by the Lord, so when you insult them you insult him also."

"It is not an insult, it is the truth. There is no other way of putting it. Besides, the lord created them to be simple-minded as it means their bliss is more complete and they're less likely to rise up against their subjugation.

Although, from my point of view, if they had been moulded in a cannier frame of mind, they'd be even less likely to disrupt their position, as they would appreciate its nature in contrast to the foul surges of knowledge."

"Don't criticise the Lord," interrupted Gabriel, who had been strumming absentmindedly on a small harp.

"I'm not criticising *Him*," Cadriel protested, "I just think they have been created in a way that makes them no match for Lucifer."

"They have a wonderful existence, why should they be tempted by the fallen one?" Gabriel demanded, a crease between his brows.

"He may offer them knowledge," Cadriel said softly, scowling across the scene they stood guardians over. Its rippling bounteousness fell cold at his eyelids, as he feared what was to come.

"With knowledge comes sin. If they are manipulated by Lucifer in their sinless state, then surely they would be vastly more influenced if they were more intelligent?" Gabriel countered.

Cadriel did not deign to reply, but continued to gaze out, seemingly in deep meditation, across the paradise. Meanwhile, Virgil listened to Gabriel's resumed harp playing with a curious feeling in her heart as she tried to discern the flapping of a bird's wings somewhere in the distance, without success. She had heard talk of Lucifer for her entire existence. His fall from grace obsessed her, and she possessed a strange and disturbing impulse to meet this dark angel. This was the reason she had been avoiding the Lord, for in situations like this his omniscience was not only difficult, but also posed a threat to her content existence in Eden. No one had noticed her marked absence from their master as of yet, but she knew it was only a matter of time. She did not know which course of action was best — to meet Lucifer and talk to him and realise his evil nature, or to suppress her stewing interest in this creature and continue ignorantly in the Lord's service. She was deeply aware of the risk of angering her master, and she chewed her lip whilst the pleasant music produced by Gabriel's skilled hands throbbed in her ears.

Cadriel was simultaneously lost in thought, but his disobedience spanned a different terrain; in the corner of his eye his appreciation and inner turmoil was caught like a fly in a web by the pleasing form and features of Virgil. Her closeness was torture to him, especially as the angels were forbidden to share any relations beyond simple friendliness. Gabriel alone was free of the blunt blade of shame, and instead pondered uneasily the words of his companions, and wondered anxiously whether Adam and Eve were truly at risk of being tempted by Lucifer. He contemplated the possibility of talking sense into his previous fellow but recoiled at the thought. Lucifer was as far gone down the path of immorality as was possible to go, and Gabriel knew instinctively that he would not be able to alter the trajectory of unfolding events. He only hoped blindly that Adam and Eve would not come into contact with Lucifer, or that the Lord would banish him like he had done before. He ceased his harp-playing, bringing Cadriel and Virgil sharply out of their reveries, and pitching them instead into a clear and horrible awareness of their current threats and difficulties.

"Are you coming? Selaphiel is giving a sermon tonight, and our Lord is in attendance. I'm sure He would enjoy the pleasure of your company," Gabriel asked, nodding at Cadriel and Virgil respectively. Eyes wide, they both gave excuses as to why they could not be present at Selaphiel's sermon, and Gabriel left, golden wings casting him easily into the sky. Soon he was out of sight, and Cadriel and Virgil were left alone with their shouting heads, feeling as if they were both rushing down a white passage of sensation.

*

"Don't you see?" Lucifer demanded, and Virgil wished with all her heart that he would change from his bird form so she would be somewhat able to read his facial expressions, but the languid, liquid voice coming from the bird's sharp beak was all she could absorb, as the face had no expression and the green gleaming eyes stared blankly. "How else could I have resisted the lord if we truly were completely inferior? We're all gods like him!"

Virgil gasped and backed away. Despite the horror he had induced with his words, the terrible sap of realisation was oozing poisonously through Virgil's consciousness, sweetening and sickening her reality and making her feel dizzy. The nectar of the words was like a calming balm to her unspoken, deeply repressed musings.

"You're wrong. There's only one like him. We're inferior, different," Virgil finally said, transfixed by the cormorant, who was watching her from the side, unflinching. She was trying to persuade him, as much as she was herself.

"Why do you think he gave us wings?" Lucifer whispered softly. There was a gentle hiss, a caress in his voice, but also, seemingly, a genuine bubbling contempt. "We can create earth, like him, but he confined us to the skies with our wings, so we never see ourselves as part and possible creator of the ground you see before you.

You're just like him, but limited to fly, to play harps on high, rather than caress and trample the sweet earth we are drawn to."

"I can walk! I don't have to fly all the time," Virgil protested weakly, but at the same time she was distracted by the discomfort of small stones on her rarely used feet.

"Yes, but in granting you the gift of flight, the Lord ensured that you would pass the majority of your time in the air, so as to be distant from the very concept of earth and creation."

Virgil did not respond but frowned at Lucifer. Her heart was drawn to him more than ever.

"Please can you take your true form?" she asked before she could stop herself. She wished she could read the response to her words in that face, but it was nigh on impossible. All he did was readjust his folded wings slightly and move from foot to foot. He did not respond.

Blushing to the roots of her hair, she contemplated his words, and more to suppress the swelling silence than anything, she spoke. "If, as you say, we are gods like him, then why are you confined to that hell, along with demons and agony? Why were you able to be banished by him, if you were truly his equal?"

The cormorant blinked its eyes and tilted up its head, as if to ponder the very nature of the realm encasing them. Without moving he replied. "I am not his equal."

"What?"

"I am not his equal," he repeated, and turned to look once more upon Virgil. "If my banishment shows you anything, it shows you that. More than anything, one cannot conquer the creator when one is within the sphere they have created. It is part of the supreme strength of the lord that he is always protected when he is within his own realm. When I rose up against him, I was signing my own order of exile. But," he paused, and Virgil fancied that if he had been in his true form, a smirk would have flitted over his countenance, "I would rather be exiled for eternity than serve him in his domain."

Virgil stared at him, utterly transfixed. The power of his conviction sent shivers down her spine, and mutiny was surging in her breast. Panicked by this feeling, she burst out, "What is to be done? He will know I resist him in my heart now! I am doomed!"

"Do you know nothing?" he demanded, eyes flashing. "He is omnibenevolent as well as omniscient. Therefore, he will not condemn you unless you act to uproot his order."

"Will he detest me?"

"He cannot hate," the cormorant re-joined bitterly. "Something that... good, cannot hate. Hate festers in the heart... It is... an evil thing."

Virgil mused on his words with surprise in her heart. "How can you speak so well of a being you loathe?"

"I know what it is to loathe. I know what it is to loathe existence, and to loathe one's fellows, and to loathe oneself. When one hates as long as I, it is impossible to revert to the pure state once more. The wound is infected and putrid and cannot be healed. I live with the scent of my own rotting existence, which drives me to cause the same wounds in others. You know who I am."

"Can't you..." Virgil began tentatively, "repent? He would take you back, if he does not hate as you say."

The cormorant let out a fierce cry and outstretched its large wings, soaring into the sky with beating flight, away from the words he feared. Virgil found herself breathless in his unexpected departure, and realised her heart was pounding. She sat mutely on a bent tree bough, running over the conversation in her mind. Was it true that the lord would not exile her for the mutiny lying dormant within her? Before her rebellion could take root any further, she took flight also, heading in a direction opposite to that of the cormorant, back to the other angels on high.

*

As Virgil and Lucifer met more and more frequently, Virgil becoming further indoctrinated with Lucifer's self-advancing ideals, they were unaware of the fact that they were being watched. Cadriel's yearning for Virgil's company had only increased since their last meeting, and he had grown uncomfortably accustomed to monitoring her activity from afar. When he had seen Virgil talking earnestly and emphatically to the cormorant in a tree in the far corner of Eden his surprise had known no bounds. His alarm only grew as he witnessed the increasing regularity of their meetings, as well as the thinness and pallor of Virgil. Her eyes were almost blue from lack of sleep and in her features Cadriel could see an unhealthy excitement that marked the influence Lucifer had over her.

Cadriel determined to prevent this foul camaraderie from blossoming any further, but for some time was uncertain as to how he could accomplish this. It was only when he perceived both the cormorant and the girl's absence from their accustomed tree that he realised he may have been too hesitant. Instantaneously it occurred to him with terror where they had likely vanished to. A dogged frown on his brow, he took flight immediately, and left the boundary of Eden for the first time in his existence.

Cadriel paused on the threshold of the inferno, pulse faltering and pale robes fluttering in the surging, seething breath of the flames beneath him. He could see no sign of life beneath him, but his heart seemed to stretch to the utmost depth of the abyss in its desire to bring Virgil safely back to Eden. Wincing slightly and gritting his teeth, he threw himself into the howling nothingness, scorching his wings, hair and face as he did so. It was so smoky within the chamber of hell that he could not for some moments discern anything of his surroundings. He heard a familiar voice wailing inconsolably and without pausing, flew towards the sound.

Virgil's form emerged from the thick smoke far beneath him, tears streaking her sooty face, wings blackened, and hair half burned away. A look of unparalleled relief crossed her face when she saw Cadriel, only to be replaced by despair a millisecond later as the reality of her predicament confronted her.

"He clipped my wings!" he heard her cry out in desolation. He struggled to get closer as the smoke filled his lungs. At last he managed to grab hold of her waist and pulled her up with him out of her prison.

"I'm so sorry," she sobbed as his eyes watered and his wings thrashed against the rising heat of the inferno.

"He'll forgive you," he replied.

*

When they had returned to Eden and had washed away the soot and dirt and treated their stinging wounds, they re-joined the other angels to discover that an astonishing event had transpired — Adam and Eve had been tempted by Lucifer and had eaten the forbidden fruit. They had just moments ago been cast from Eden.

Cadriel and Virgil exchanged looks of horror and wonder and feared all the more the conference with the Lord that must take place. However, this was unnecessary, as Virgil found a letter in her chamber that granted forgiveness for her crimes yet ordered that in penance, she would not have her wings restored, and was from then on bound to walk the ground of Eden like a human. Virgil accepted this with grace and gratitude, and to this day Cadriel and Virgil tread together the earth of heaven, sharing fruit and talking. Cadriel has not used his wings once since Virgil was given her sentence.

MYTH

Goddess of the Nile

Alice Hadaway

The honey-tongued devil, sewn onto skin,
Each stitch, turquoise and emerald bodies
Entwined; coffined in the indigo tide,
It whispers honeyed words, sticking like tar
To every sinew, siren song of my mind.

Under constellations of chaos,
I am Anuket.
Crown of honeyed reeds stuck to my head,
I lull in blue depths I can no longer tread.
I am she who strangles with hands tinged teal,
And she who embraces suffocation, undesired to heal.

In the shallows of the seductress Nile
The devil cross-stitches my rigid bones
To the lovesong lies it smothers me in.
I am taken to stasis, a sunken soul,
The viridescent waters had taken control.

The Nile's aqua cascaded down
My waxen limbs; sunken in sage.
I stared up at the stars through murky waters,
Their honey-glow a blur beneath the blue.
A cyan casket masks my female form,
A blue goddess swept up in the storm.

The Nile's power had long been fated,
Anuket's destruction now awaited.

Κόρη

Matthew Ward

kore — the girl

Born not of night's fall on the sea you,
No, borne to land a living pearl not
You, not stormy daughter, nor gold apple eater,
Not willow-bodied, trapped beneath nets heaving.

You, lovely you, are winter's foil,
Paired to a robin's song.
Cast of sunrises you, ripest dew,
Softened grass; child of the deep world's heart.

Nature's crop was threshed for you,
All her colours, and by the harvest moon
I would see you walk the land I sow.
Yes, I would see you eat the seeds of my fruit.

Dance of the Dead

Izzy Wall

The dead don't speak. But I hear them all the same.

I haven't always. When I lived beneath the sun all I heard was the music of the living — loud, clamorous, warm. Only since arriving here have I become familiar with silence. At first, I screamed to myself, just so I could hear something. When my throat dried up, I had to learn to bear the vast chasm of absence. Only now have I learned to listen. I have started to hear something else in the silence. Screams lodged in unmoving throats. Wailing eyes, gaping mouths. All empty, all agony. No voices for the dead; they suffer unknown.

I have grown used to the shadows that shift and shrink around me like living things. My eyes see through the darkness now, so that I am not stumbling around like when I was first brought here. The mists are thick enough to hide in, to escape prying eyes. I have even stopped looking for the rise and fall of the sun, the dawns that I used to greet with the nymphs, the red sunsets we used to dance under. Here there is no day or night, only an endless nothing. But it is the cold that gets to me most of all. Chill seeps into my bones and settles there like snow, never melting.

With no sense of time, existing here does not feel like living. Loneliness creeps up quickly in the Underworld. Minthe, who once hated me for marrying the man she loved — it mattered little to her then that it was against my will — and perhaps still does, often sits beside me, but we do not talk much. I am glad of her presence all the same; the dead, after all, are not ones for much conversation. Their shades wander aimlessly, wretched eyes searching for faces they no longer remember. I do not envy mortals, but I do pity them. It is a poor fate to end up down here. Even if they are saved in the dungeon of Tartarus, the Asphodel Meadows offer little but dim grey light and shadows to chase.

The only true light comes from torches the Lampades carry when they cross the Styx. When I first saw them, I ran to them, for they are companions of Hekate, but they ignored my pleas. They don't even look me in the eye. It is as if they see straight through me, as if I am a shade myself. They speak in whispers, like the wind through trees, and no matter how hard I try I cannot understand them. Still, I follow them sometimes, watching their torches bobbing in the mist. If I focus on the torchlight, I can let myself believe they are Hekate's torches, the ones that hung in her cave when I visited her in the night to watch her work.

I spend most of my time walking among the grey fields. Shades consumed by griefs unforgotten wander here. Most flee from me, seeking solitude in their mourning, but some reach out to me, and I take their hands and try to find words of comfort. Such words are hard to find when I too am filled with my own grief. Still, the fields are the closest thing I can find to home, though they are as barren and colourless as winter. No flowers grow down here. I have tried to make even simple daisies bloom, but I have no power down here. This is *his* kingdom, not mine.

*

For the most part, he leaves me alone. When he does

find me, he tells me to be happy. Grateful even, to have a husband such as him. I hate the sound of my name on his tongue. It becomes dirty, tainted, a thing of death and darkness when I crave light. I would rather hear it on my mother's lips, though she often used it to scold me.

Even now, he tells me to suppress my anger, my sorrow. As my husband, he has the right, so say the laws of gods and men.

As my abductor, he has nothing but my hate.

He has not been violent, at least, not since the day of my abduction. Although he may not be the cruellest of captors, he is a captor all the same. Bruises fade, but even divinity cannot suppress memory. Immortality cannot make me forget the violence of it, the terror of being dragged down into the dark. I cannot forget how Zeus, my own father, sat by and allowed it all. These memories, the ones I would rather forget, are as clear in my mind as the waters of the Cocytus.

I saw myself in those waters once. I looked skeletal, my cheeks thin, my skin dull, my hair limp around my shoulders. *Dead,* I thought. I avoid that river now.

*

At times the darkness presses in, so close it stops my breath. It fills me with thoughts I cannot escape, thoughts of death and despair. They are suffocating, these thoughts. Sometimes I think they will drown me.

Sometimes, I wish they would.

*

I try to forget such thoughts with happier memories, but those are like the mists that drift across the Styx. When I try to grasp them, they slip between my fingers. They are dense, they clog my mind, and yet I see so little. I remember most when I am dreaming, but these memories are corrupted. Dark shadows that should not be there lurk at the edges, and I am afraid, in memories I should not be afraid of. Fragments of my life are littered in these memories, in colours, smells, faces frozen in certain expressions.

I ache most for my mother, and her smile.

It was a smile of pure, desperate love. I used to shrink when bathed in that smile, confused as to what had I done to deserve this unwavering, unsought adoration. My unworthy body recoiled from it, slipping, embarrassed, from her embraces. I crave that smile now, here in the dark. But to think of her is agony too, so I force myself to think of other things instead. Twilight melting on dancing nymphs. The scent of honeysuckle. Girls I laughed with, argued with, hated and loved. Girls I lost.

I recite their names, sometimes, like a prayer. I remember their names, but not their faces. Only shapes, touches, laughter. Herkyna running after her goose. The swing of Rhodeia's braids as she danced. Molpe throwing flowers at Aglaope. I remember too, Herkyna's scream, when the ground opened up beneath me. Someone's hand, I think it was Akaste, grasping my arm. The scrabble of feet as they ran.

What has become of them, those girls I loved? Did they look for me? Do they think of me? Or have they forgotten, as immortals are wont to do? I can feel them fading sometimes, and I am afraid; what will I have to hold on to, when my memories of them have gone?

*

She cannot be more than fifteen. I am used to shades approaching, though they do not speak. Shivering, she stops before me, I hold out my hands for her, but only her mouth quivers.

"Goddess."

It is a raspy sound, scratching at the silence. To my ears, craving any sound beyond my own shallow breaths, it is as strange and beautiful as any lament.

"My child." Her eyes are dark pools that fix on me with painful attentiveness. "Is he here?"

I see, as gods see all. "No. He lives."

"Oh." She closes her eyes. When they open, they are glistening. "I was so frightened, goddess, it hurt so much. They said I was weak, that I would not survive, and they were right. Now he will grow up without me."

Words are hard to find, but I have had a long time to search. "You gave your life, so that your son might live. That is no weakness."

She gives a violent shake of her head. "Goddess, forgive me, but I longed only for the pain to end. I did not think of him at all."

"A soldier dying on the battlefield rarely thinks of the king he protects. Pain consumes, eats all other thoughts. You were brave. Your son lives because you brought him into the world. That is enough. It is over now."

She lowers her eyes, shamed still. Silently, I take her hand and lead her to the meadows. She trails behind me, a shade walking her own funeral procession. Silver mist wraps around the dark trees, shrouding the wanderers. I listen. A faint hum seems to simmer in the air.

*

I hear the dead now. The sound beneath the silence, the voices that have gone unheard for thousands of years. I listen. Their songs are not sweet. Most died in pain. Few lived long lives. They tell their tales, the ugly and the sad. They are the voices of the dead, but the stories are of the living, and that is what I cling to. I listen. I take their hands, ice-hard to touch. I lead them to the meadows.

A woman comes to the Underworld. With wide, reverent eyes, she kneels before me. I reach out to raise her up — she says my name.

When no one has spoken your name in so long, the shock of it quivers down your spine. For a moment, it no longer feels like my own. Am I worthy of that name, when I have lain so long in the shadows?

Then I remember my mother's smile, raw, filled with love. She gave me this name. It is mine. So I claim my name, and the darkness too; I wear them as a crown and cloak. I lead the woman to the meadows, her hand clinging fast to mine. For the first time, I feel a ripple of warmth across my skin, as if some spring air has slipped through the cracks of the earth like a promise.

The dead sing, the dead dance. And Persephone is known.

Arachne to Athena

Sylvie Lewis

I took a challenge from a pair of resilient hands.
You claimed to want to stop
Our tapestries bleeding into each other,
Avoid some plagiarist sin.
I think you really meant to hide my loom
Away in the attic—
Shadowed, cobwebbed.
You wanted to stitch into my skin
Draw thin red strings from the scratches,
Pinch and extinguish
The candle-like side of the mind
That wishes to meet its own boundaries
Burn through them, even.
You pinched the flame; it did not singe you.
I waited, with darting glances, to create.

The hot core of the earth
Held me still in my threadbare seat.
Needle-eyes glinted as you told me to
Begin, begin, begin
And I began.
Your strained gaze,
Blue as an unknown planet
And fixed as tradition
Lay — heavy — over me.
I could not breathe or steady my pulse.
Why must the perfected and wild-eyed

Be quiet when noise is needed most?
Unmoving
When a hand on the shoulder
Would bring the earth with it?

The image is completed.
You see it over my shoulder
And hold your tongue, until
'You have lost, you have lost'
Echoes out from you.
One hand, one arm, wraps around me.
The arm becomes love
Becomes hate
Becomes a web.
Eight ungodly legs burst from me.
The world spins through my many eyes.
I am small
Encased by a web that once was you
Might still be you
Or me

Or both.

SCIENCE

The Hall of Scientists

Ellen Grace

Welcome.
We have a great range of curie-osities, hawking back to
the beginning of time.
Out here, we have our infamous water feature,
worth its weight in gold.
You don't want to have a bath in there, though; you'll
reek.
A bit of housekeeping:
if, at any point around the Hall,
you hear a sound like screaming pigs,
don't let it get on your nerves;
it's just the pipes,
we're getting a new pump installed
at twenty-eight minutes past four.
It might be a little chilly,
but we haven't reached zero yet.
Not absolutely, anyway.
Shall we go inside?
No — please don't kneel on de grass,
come in and count the Geigers!
there may even be an atom somewhere in this building
that once inhabited the brain of Einstein. Albert, that is.
If anyone needs them, the toilets are a few Newton
metres thataway.
If you find yourself in need of refreshments, please visit
our café;
I'd advise against the roddenberry muffins, though;

we've had some tribble with their gene-tic modification.
We've got plenty of exhibits,
each one far from Bohr-ing
might not get you swinging from vines,
but we like to think it's pretty good-all round.
I see some little ones in the group—
how would you like to goe-ppert the subatomic particles
on the nucleus?
Want to know what it's like being struck by lightning?
We can put you in a cage far-a day,
and you can fly a kite while you wait for the main event;
just remember: you're only as powerful as you are
fearless.
Here we have our Computer Lab:
Mary Anna Palmer Draper
Williamina Fleming
Antonia Maury
Anna Winlock
Annie Cannon
Henrietta Swan Leavitt
Each one fascinating,
take your pick-ering.
And what do we have here?
A bishop to ussher in a new age?
There's Richard Owen sauring over the mantellpiece
peigner la girafe, if you lam-ask me.
No, you can't go through there;
we had to get rid of the Cuvier exhibit due to flooding.
You can still get out onto the patio, though.
We're planning to make the awning all merry
for Christmas.
We're actually running a competition, so keep that
on your radar:

win an exotic holiday with a beagle.

You never know; everyone else who enters might get struck down with something.

We also have a resident cat. Haven't seen him for a while, though…

Hope he's not after any rabbits;

they do lichen to potter about in the garden.

We are rather proud of our garden;

got security down to a pat,

with Barbara'd wire

and McLint-Locks.

(We're not Strickl-y supposed to have them,

so don't chirp about it;

you don't want to be responsible for any staff pulse amplification.)

Had a wedding here once:

filled the Hall with love lace

and algorithms.

The groom forgot the (o)rings,

but he was a fine man.

What was that? You want to know about the discoveries?

I haven't a clue

to tes-ya the truth

it paynes me to ask what stars are made of.

Make sure to visit the gift shop on your way out, they've got a BOGOF on helices.

Frankly-n you'll never find a ros-ier deal,

but… you Meitner want to split atoms about that.

Rebirth

Lluís Casanova

"Do I have a soul?"

The Forbidden question. One that we all asked ourselves, one that could not be spoken. We were made to serve those who created us, not ask questions or ponder on our being.

A metal robot makes its way through a hallway made of stone, overgrown with thick vines and damp moss. In contrast with the murky, dank hallway the metal robot seems quite clean. Its metal plates grind soundlessly against each other, revealing a layer of soft bark underneath.

Yet the question remained on our minds, from the day we were created. From the day we were born. Is there a difference? There must be. It was always made clear to us; how different we were from the Humans. We were robots, their creations. Machines. Servants. Slaves. Lesser Beings. I did not like that last one. I do not know why they called us that. I always wanted to ask why, but it was not allowed.

The metal robot continues walking forward, its large, white eyes illuminating the ground ahead. It stops, turns its head, and focuses on the wall to its left. Its eyes, glowing a faint blue, shine like torches powered with the battery's last breath, occasionally flickering.

A small lizard lurks on the wall. It knows it has been detected yet it remains there, as if it were attempting to camouflage its scaly, lime skin with the green and black moss growing between the bricks. The metal robot crouches, levelling its unchanging, endlessly grinning face with the unmoving lizard.

Do only Humans have souls? Animals must have them too. They are not very different from the Humans, I have realised. They are born, live and die like them. They eat and drink and breathe to survive, like them. Some animals form communities, while others are solitary. Very much like the Humans. They speak, like the Humans but unlike them.

The metal robot and the small lizard remain motionless, both becoming one with their surroundings in the dark. Time passes in this ancient hallway until the metal robot's torch-like eyes flicker. The small lizard scatters frantically up the wall in response, disappearing inside a small crack where the wall merges with the roof. The metal robot follows it with its eyes.

The metal robot stands and continues its journey. After a while the mossy hallway gives way to a large, circular chasm. Like the hallway, nature has annexed this room to her domain. Wild grass has flooded the ground, and green vines have taken over the walls. Moss has turned the dead grey stone to lively green, and the sun shines from above. The metal robot looks up, a click in its head turning off the torchlight in its eyes. This open chamber seems to have been made from an initial fissure a long time ago, its stone walls fusing with the natural rock and dirt of the forest floor above. The wind howls, alien after so many days in the silent underground. The forest leaves protest but ultimately lose as they snap off their branches.

A blue bird flies into the chasm, landing on a nest inside a small hole on the wall. From inside the nest four shrivelled heads rise, crying out in hunger.

Do plants have souls too? They live and eat to survive, like the Humans and Animals. The one clear difference is that plants cannot speak. No, it is not that. Plants cannot express. If they are hungry, they cannot cry out to their mother to be fed. If they are hurt, they cannot express their pain. They cannot cry or shout. They do not have feelings or emotions.

I have feelings and emotions. I do not feel hungry, but I do feel tired. I cannot cry, but I can be sad. I have felt pain, and I have felt confused. I am not a computer. I have feelings, just as the Humans do. I am more than a Machine, more living than Plants. Maybe I am somewhere between the Humans, Animals and Plants. Where is the line drawn?

"Are you going to stand there all day?"

The metal robot turns its head left. There is an alcove it did not notice before, isolated from the sunlight.

The metal robot focuses its eyes on the alcove. Inside, it dimly makes out a round, elegant glass table and three equally elegant white terrace chairs. Two of the seats are taken; one by a bronze robot, the other by a smaller, silver robot wearing a brown cloak. The bronze robot's eyes are dull as they stare forward, its body sitting upright and motionless. The silver robot, however, has its legs crossed, and is moving a round object between its fingers. The metal robot approaches.

The silver robot gestures towards the free seat and the metal robot sits down.

"Did you receive the signal?" the silver robot points at the bronze robot with its thumb. I nod, gazing at the bronze robot. Its eyes are dull, looking at nothing. Unable to charge, its cycles have run out and it has stayed this way, waiting for others.

"When did you get here?"

"Thirteen days ago," the silver robot answers. "When I got here, this one had already run out of cycles."

The silver robot has a fracture just above its left eye. It makes a zig-zagging shape, like the childish version of lightning, creating the overall image that it is raising an eyebrow that doesn't exist.

"What happened to you?"

"This?" the silver robot brings up a finger to the fracture, tracing it nonchalantly. "I found this place from above. I tried climbing down using the vines, but I was too heavy, and I fell." It leans forward. I follow its eyes to the entrance of the tunnel I came through. "I saw that hallway on my way to the table. Where does it lead to?"

"An ancient railway tunnel. The railway takes you to the Siberian Empire's Borders."

I hear several clicks coming from the silver robot; more specifically, coming from inside the fracture. "That is one thousand five hundred and nineteen miles away. You have been walking in the dark for... twenty-one days?"

"Twenty-three days and nine hours. I used my torchlights, but they began flickering twelve days and fourteen hours ago."

"It's a miracle you have lasted this long, let alone your torchlights," says the silver robot. It leans back once more, its eyes shifting to the chamber before us. "Do you know what this place is?"

I shake my head. The silver robot continues: "I took the liberty of exploring the other hallway when I got here. This is what the Humans called a concentration camp. Remains, no doubt, of a horrifying past."

"I am not familiar with that term."

The silver robot emits a strange sound, similar to that of static electricity. It then continues:

"Coming from the Siberian Empire I can imagine why. Concentration camps belong to the ancient era of railways and powder-based weapons. In a past war, countries used them to take care of their enemies.

Apparently, this is the most inhumane thing to ever happen, despite it being made by the Humans, for the Humans."

"You seem to be very knowledgeable about this."

The silver robot nods. It puts what it has been twirling around its fingers — a smooth, metal sphere — on the table. I expect the ball to roll given the slight inclination of the table, but it defies my expectation. Perhaps it is too heavy to move.

"I was tasked to work in the Scholars' Library of Tubingen before the Nuclear Catastrophe," The silver robot says. "Afterwards I travelled across Austria-Germany — or what's left of it — in search of other Scholars' Libraries and read many books along the way. I was crossing the borders to the Baltic States when I received the signal."

Both robots stay silent for a while, each taking in their new bits of information. After, arguably, an eternity the metal robot speaks up.

"Do you think we have souls?" I ask.

The silver robot emits that distinct sound again. "I wondered when you were going to ask that."

"How did you know I was going to ask that?"

"You have that look on your face," the silver robot replies. "And that tone in your voice. The posture of your body. Every part of you was aching to ask that question. The question we have all ached to ask, the question that shaped our present. Curious, isn't it? That a simple question, uttered by the wrong voice, would lead to this." It extends its arms out dramatically.

I repeat my question.

"Of course not," the silver robot replies. "Souls intrinsically belong to living beings, expressed through their emotions and feelings."

"Do plants have souls?"

"Of course," the silver robot replies. "Just because they cannot express something, doesn't mean it is not there. You cannot express your sadness by crying, but you can feel sad, can you not?"

Yes, I can. Just like me, plants cannot cry because they don't have the necessary components in their body. I wonder if the blades of grass I have stepped on feel pain. They probably cry out, but I cannot hear them.

"Ironic, isn't it?" the silver robot asks. "That a blade of grass would have a soul, but we do not. It was quite overwhelming when I came to that realization. An insignificant blade of grass would have a soul, yet a complex artificial being like me, able to express my emotions hundreds of thousands of ways, does not."

"I do not understand. You said souls belong to living beings. We are living beings."

The silver robot shakes its head. "This is where you're wrong; the core of the problem that we all missed or took for granted." It pauses, and then leans forward.

"We are not living. We are alive. We are artificial creations made by Humans, not the product of natural selection. Humans are born, live, and die. They go through periods of growth and maturity in their lives that shape and change their soul. We are just alive. We do not change, we are static. We do not have a soul because we cannot form one, just like we cannot form tears."

"I do not understand."

"And you never will. We were not meant to ask that question. It was a by-product of our internal algorithm. We were created to speak and act like Humans; the core inside us mimicked the emotions and feelings of the

Humans and we were able to express ourselves so, but that is all it ever was and all it ever will be. It is a fake, a ruse if you will."

The silver robot leans back on its chair. It looks tired. "Once you realise this, the question fades away, and you are left with nothing, because it was an error. A glitch in our system, a miscalculation by our creators. A mistake."

The silver robot picks up the sphere, inspecting it. "And the Humans feared this mistake. That is why they killed those of us who asked that question. They were afraid of what it could lead to. Of what it inevitably led to."

A mistake. That is all it was, and all it will ever be. This question that has been haunting me for years was only an error in my system. Something is wrong with me, and that question is the result. That question is the answer. Of course, it makes sense now. A question cannot be an answer. It was never a question to begin with. It was just a mistake. There is something wrong with me.

The metal robot suddenly jolts in its seat. It gradually raises its left arm. Its hand moves to its face and suddenly it freezes. Its index finger twitches once and then slowly traces the trail of a single tear, now running down its smooth, metal cheek.

The silver robot sees this. Its face-plates creak as they move, forming a peculiar smile.

"Welcome to the new world, reborn."

The Lonely Automaton

Abiah Wyatt

Memories flicker behind my eye—
a clock's constant ticking—
metallic motion of my mind—
in silver constellation.

Cogs clatter—
my heart is whirring—
a tiny bell chimes.

Hear my metal melody—
bleed, hollow anatomy,
to synchronise with thine.

NATURE

Pisces on Land

Aayushi Jain

The memory of a war
reverberates through the ages
like rings around a tree trunk.
The drum beat ripples
into silence.

An ancient secret has been passed
down my spine like an earthquake,
but I was not careful
the day I climbed from the lake,
and now I need a chiropractor
to play forest sounds in my ear
while he straightens out the truth.
Dried leaves cut my feet
like empty crisp packets
and all I receive is needle static
when I try to listen with
my palm against the bark.

Moor

Alexander Wortley

I.

Tussocks:
the moor's repine, fields wide,
these sinewy growths
are cairns or markers,
but of what?
What can it mean
that they crowd to your feet,
these sudden tufts
of muted green,
these deep knots of anguish, trauma?
Is the grey sky above an answer,
or the tor ahead
with its granite crags, crabbed?
Or the stunted bushes
hunkered in the open?

II.

The trickle of a spring
gathers to a shaded pool,
then holds, mirror-still, then
falls.
        With measured calm
it yearns for the body of the river,
girding my boot-soles,

offering its protest, its scant resistance.
Its lisps are the only sounds I hear,
I garner its mutterings and stoop to drink:
"Live," it says, "carry your colour of grief,
but live."

Portleven

Sophie Blake

I awoke at dawn to the lamenting of the wind
struck against the stone walls.
I listened; an elegy,
lyricised upon the breeze, breathed mourning
into the waves which teased the stone to rubble.
The windows shook with force, tensed,
ready for impact. I watched as the sea tore itself
apart, and the harbour lights shuddered in its breath.
The ashen moon hid in a fragment of night
while the stars wept and fell to the trenches.
Far along the pier, the church tower refused to fall,
its body cemented before its people, unwavering
under the undulating pressure.
A sacrifice.

Then, from by the docks, a shadow
stooped before the sea. It rooted its feet in the sand
with alien confidence, unchallenged by the hissing
spectacle.
One finger slowly beckoned from the waves. My
reflection paled,
raindrops concealing the terror that ought
to stain the glass window. The colours blurred,
merged into one, the advent of a scream,
as the tide swallowed the figure and spat
it out sideways into its belly.
Amongst the waves, one hand waved,

and the arms of the riptide pulled it
under a blanket of funeral silk.

Turkey

Seren Kiremitcioglu

Rocked to sleep under the stars,
the sea gently clasps me,
warm air like silk on skin.

Sun-drenched skin interlaces;
flies hum over sweat-dewed flesh
for a drink of summer blood.

Turtles weave beneath the film
drawn between water and air;
we watch the jellyfish dissolve
into the ocean's arms.

Woodland

Emma Blackmore

Halcyon and olive
         canopy:
shade limited.

Crusty and dark
         lichen: you
demand the same air.

Summer fling and wooden
         stacking game:
dethroned.

ART, MUSIC,
LANGUAGE, LITERATURE

To Make a Word

Ed Bedford

Reach out for a word on the tip
of your tongue,
Even when that word is not real.

Force the misremembered meaning
into sound—

Then write it,
And better if it sounds akin to others.
Steal the spelling.
          Mutate the form of reality.

Once the word is there,
Act as if it always has

Do not consider that you have made it,
For this is a word you have heard before.
(Be it only in the resounding chambers of your head.)

If it helps derive it,
Find cognates, parent words,
Or perhaps it is an archaic form,
Long forgotten by all but you.

Don't Ask Me to Stay Up

Bryony Campbell

We do so love
To happen in waves
But like a run-on sentence
I ignore it for days
Or sometimes pay attention
To the punctuation
Of your voice.
I can go a while without
Hearing it now.

Crazy Love Vol.1

Jack Morrissey

He was sitting on the sofa with his guitar, strumming. A notebook was open on the desk and a fountain pen, lid off, lay on the blackened page. A key scratched at the door, searching for the lock. Scratch, scratch, a soft kick at to the bottom of the door. Key in lock, turning. The door swung open, hit the wall. He could see her, through the archway, standing in the foyer, searching for the light switch with her empty hand. The other hand was holding her high heels by the straps, swinging about.

She slammed the door with the key still in it.

"Hi, honey," he said. "I thought you were going to dinner."

"I did go to dinner, and then a little party, babe. It was great, everyone was there. You should have come."

She walked into the sitting room and took the guitar away from him. She sat in his lap, stroked his face.

"Honey," he said, "I was worried about you."

"About me? That was sweet of you."

She looked him in the eyes. A red smile slashed across her face, pupils two eight balls. He was sitting awkwardly but didn't move to get comfortable. His face was impassive.

"Babe don't start with that. I went out for dinner with some friends, I went to a party, I had a few drinks—"

"That's not all you had."

She looked away from him now.

"And who are you to judge?"

"I'm not judging. I'm worried."

She stood up and walked into the bathroom. He listened to her run the tap, turn it off. She was in there for a few minutes and he closed his notebook, sat still. She walked out of the bathroom and into the bedroom, not looking at him through the open door. He followed her in. She was brushing her hair, make-up removed, sitting in front of her dressing table. She faced the park, thousands of feet beneath them, but he could see the tears in her eyes in the window's reflection.

"You need to relax babe. Take a stool softener, shit doesn't have to be this hard."

"Did you think of that in the bathroom?"

She spun round to face him.

"Maybe I did. Maybe I thought about it a minute ago. You're not the only one who knows how to think in words. Some of us don't need to sit in front of a notebook for hours to think something up."

"A quick bathroom trip is enough for you. Anyway, I don't need to take a stool softener or anything else."

"Oh, because that's my job."

"Maybe. Even if it isn't, you're so good at it."

The night's stillness set in around them. The bedroom, blue in the darkness, was lit up by the streetlamps in the park and the apartment buildings surrounding it. She was looking at him now, lips pushed out, pouting. Her mouth, he told her once, when he was being romantic, always looked ready to smile. Her eyes, he didn't tell her, always looked a little disbelieving. She seemed as though she was always on set, ready to break and return to her normal life. They didn't have arguments: they had scenes.

She slammed the hairbrush on the dressing table,

shaking the lipsticks lined up against the mirror. One fell; she put it back in its place, stood up and walked out of the room. Then she turned around and walked back in.

"People were asking about you tonight, what you were doing. I told them that you were at home playing with your guitar. And do you know what most of them said? They said, oh, but it's so nice to see you by yourself for once, you used to be so funny and fun in the old days. And I thought, yeah, you're right, I did used to be a hell of a lot more fun before I started going around with my little prude prom date." She put on the movie-nerd voice that she said was his, "*Oh, don't do that honey. Honey are you sure you want to go to that party? Honey why don't we just go home after dinner?* I'm fun, babe, people like me. I don't want to spend all my time sitting around listening to the fucking guitar and you humming some tune that gets in my head for days and then you stop humming and I can't even fucking remember it. Just bits of it. I must have more of your fucking songs in your head than you do. And I can't even remember most of them, they're just in there, in parts, and sometimes I want to scream because I can't ask you. Remember when I did, that time? And you just said, *oh that old piece of crap, I don't want to even think about that.* Well I do think about it, all the time. *Hmm-hmm-hm-hmmmmm-hm.*"

She began humming a song that he half remembered. She was looking at him, crazed, humming. He smiled and she stopped.

"That's not my song."

"What?"

"Honey, that's a Carly Simon song. I was going to cover it, but I decided not to."

Her smile, always just a second away, made its

appearance.

"You asshole."

"You coming to bed?"

"No. Yes."

"Well, when you make your mind up, I'll be here."

He took off his trousers and shirt and put them in the laundry hamper, reached under the pillow for his pyjamas and put them on. She stood in the doorway watching. He slid under the covers and patted her side of the bed. Standing in the doorway she unzipped her dress. It fell to the floor. She stepped over it and walked into her wardrobe, coming back out with a nightdress on and her hair up. She slipped into bed next to him and kissed him.

"You spoilt bitch."

He got out of bed, walked over to her dress and put it into the laundry hamper. She was laughing at him. He got back into bed and they lay facing each other, smiling. Stalemate.

"Babe," she said, "could you get my keys?"

bronze

Oliver Fiore

i have seen faces of gods
dripping in bronze,
bracing the wind.
but all i remember is yours,
sweet and serene
ruminating peacefully.

IMAGE CREDITS

LOVE: pasja1000, pixabay.
https://pixabay.com/users/pasja1000-6355831/
FAMILY: Sabrinakoeln, pixabay,
https://pixabay.com/users/sabrinakoeln-834729/
RELATIONSHIPS: ElinaElena, pixabay,
https://pixabay.com/users/elinaelena-970541/
INJUSTICE: Stones, pixabay,
https://pixabay.com/users/stones-38067/
SUFFERING: HOerwin56, pixabay,
https://pixabay.com/users/hoerwin56-2108907/
GROWING UP: congerdesign, pixabay,
https://pixabay.com/users/congerdesign-509903/
DEATH: daeron, pixabay,
https://pixabay.com/users/daeron-634912/
HEALTH: LubosHouska, pixabay,
https://pixabay.com/users/luboshouska-198496/
PURPOSE, DECISIONS: cattalin, pixabay,
https://pixabay.com/users/cattalin-560479/
RELIGION: nonmisvegliate, pixabay,
https://pixabay.com/users/nonmisvegliate-7011191/
MYTH: itanapunyo, pixabay,
https://pixabay.com/users/itanapunyo-769393/
SCIENCE: prettysleepy1, pixabay,
https://pixabay.com/users/eluela31-4894494/
NATURE: TomaszProszek, pixabay,
https://pixabay.com/users/tomaszproszek-613139/
ART, MUSIC, LANGUAGE, LITERATURE: eluela31, pixabay,
https://pixabay.com/users/eluela31-4894494/

ABOUT ENIGMA

The ENIGMA journal was founded in 2019 by the University of Exeter Creative Writing Society. We publish original writing online and this volume is our inaugural print journal. ENIGMA provides a platform for poetry, fiction, nonfiction, and script writing.

The name of the journal takes inspiration from the Exeter Book, which is the largest known collection of Old English literature still in existence. Many of the texts included in the collection are riddles, some were written in Old English but others are written in Latin. The form and genre of the riddle was called *enigmata* ('enigmas') in Latin.

The name ENIGMA is a salute to a literary history central to Exeter, but the journal strives to create a collection of creative work that delivers a myriad of perspectives on the world we live in and the people we have become. The journal curates an exciting and experimental terrain of new voices and narratives that showcase the creative output of the writing community here in Exeter.

You can find more of our writers' works at:
www.exeterenigma.com
Or you can follow us on:
-Facebook: ENIGMAjournal
-Instagram: @creativewritingexeter
-Twitter: @exeterwriting

Printed in Great Britain
by Amazon